D1601474

THE THEOLOGICAL FOUNDATIONS OF THE MORMON RELIGION

THE
THEOLOGICAL
FOUNDATIONS
of the MORMON
RELIGION

Sterling M. McMurrin

UNIVERSITY OF UTAH PRESS • SALT LAKE CITY

Sterling M. McMurrin is E. E. Ericksen Distinguished Professor, Professor of History, Professor of the Philosophy of Education, and Dean of the Graduate School in the University of Utah.

The cover detail from
Michelangelo's Sistine Chapel ceiling
is by Dale Bryner.

To my Mother

FOREWORD

THE MOST INTERESTING THING about Mormon theology is that it incorporates a liberal doctrine of man and a radically unorthodox concept of God within the general framework of historic Christian fundamentalism. This anomaly marks the distinctive character of the theology and sets its basic problems. It provides the Mormon religion with intellectual foundations which are compatible with its biblical literalism yet support its humanistic temper. This has far-reaching implications, for, while it strengthens the naturalistic and pragmatic propensities of the Mormon people without weakening their ties to Christian origins, it must inevitably produce fundamental tensions in the intellectual life of the Church, tensions arising ultimately from the basic conflict of the Greek and Hebrew components of the culture.

The intention of this essay is to exhibit the distinctive character of Mormon theology that resides especially in the finitistic concept of God and the denial of the traditional doctrines of original sin and salvation by grace. It is based on a series of lectures delivered at the University of Utah in January and February of 1965. These were an extension of a paper titled "The Distinctive Character of Mormon Theology" read before The Utah Academy of Sciences, Arts, and Letters in 1959. The supplementary essay, "Theses on the Idea That God Is a Person," is a lecture delivered on the Great Issues Forum of the University of Utah in February 1965.

It is not my purpose here to present a systematic statement of Mormon doctrine or either to justify or criticize it. Rather I have composed a comparative commentary that is intended simply to differentiate Mormon doctrine from the classical Christian theology as that is set forth by the major theologians or expressed in certain of the historic symbols of the Christian faith. I am aware that my highly selective references to Catholic, Protestant, and Jewish doctrines and ideas can lead all too easily to distorted conceptions of those religions and their theologies. I would like to assure my readers, therefore, that my comparisons are solely in the interest of facilitating an understanding of Mormonism. I would also remind them of the great complexity and richness of historic and contemporary theology that cannot even be acknowledged in such a brief paper. Among the ideas that importantly characterize Mormon theology, I find nothing that is exclusive to it. I have made no effort here to describe the historical sources and connections of those ideas.

Mormon theology is a modern Pelagianism in a Puritan religion. Mormonism is a Judaic-like community religion grounded in the Puritan moral doctrine that the vocation of man is to create the kingdom of God. Its fundamentalism is rooted in the biblical literalism native to American religion. Its heresy is the denial of the dogma of original sin, a heresy that exhibits both the disintegration of modern Protestantism and the impact of nineteenth-century liberalism on the character of American sectarianism.

The repetition of ideas in this essay has resulted from the relative independence of the original lectures.

University of Utah, 1965   *Sterling M. McMurrin*

CONTENTS

THE THEOLOGICAL FOUNDATIONS OF THE MORMON RELIGION

PART ONE

THE CONCEPT OF REALITY

1. On Naturalism and Supernaturalism

METAPHYSICS IS AN ATTEMPT to answer the most basic
questions which can be asked concerning the nature of reality.
It has to do not with what in particular it is that in fact exists,
but rather with the nature of existence as such, or with the
general properties of whatever exists. It is concerned especially
with ontological problems on the nature of being and cosmological
problems on the structure of reality. From the Mormon scriptures
and other accepted sources, especially the officially recognized
teachings of the Mormon prophet, Joseph Smith, it is possible
to construct at least the outlines of a general conception of the
nature of reality. It is a conception that is essentially pluralistic
and materialistic, with a strong emphasis on the dynamic character
of reality and having a naturalistic and humanistic quality uncommon in theistic philosophy.

The fact of existence is basically a mystery, for an ultimate
explanation of the being of any thing or event is impossible. Traditional occidental theism explains the existence of the world by
the creative power of God, but it properly refuses to accept questions calling for an explanation of God. There is something illicit
in the demand for an explanation of the explanation. It was
typical of the ancient Greek philosophers to account for the

natural world without introducing a supernatural creative power. The existence of the natural world was simply assumed, much as typical Christian thought assumes, without explanation, the existence of a supernatural God who is the creator of nature.

Now Mormonism has much in common with the naturalistic position of the Greeks. It holds, in the first place, that although the structure and configurations of the world are the product of God's creative act, that anything at all should exist is not due to God but is simply a given fact. Just as it is the case that God exists, there are other realities as well. God is not the totality of original being and he is not the ultimate source or the creator of all being. This is a radical departure from the position of traditional theism, whether Christian, Jewish, or Islamic, and the failure to recognize the far-reaching implications of this idea is a failure to come to grips with the somewhat distinctive quality of Mormon theology, its essentially non-absolutistic character.

In the second place, the naturalistic disposition of Mormonism is found in the denial of the traditional conception of the supernatural. It is typical of Mormon writers to insist that even God is natural rather than supernatural, in that there is not a divine order of reality that contrasts essentially with the mundane physical universe of ordinary experience known to us through sensory data, which is the object of scientific investigation and is described by natural law. The naturalistic facet of Mormon thought is indicated by the Mormon denial of miracles in the traditional sense of an intrusion of the supernatural that suspends the natural processes. The typical Mormon conception of a miracle is that the miraculous event, though entirely natural, is simply not understood because of deficiencies in human knowledge. From the perspective of God there are no miracles.

The denial of the supernatural is not simply a terminological issue in Mormonism, for reality is described qualitatively as a single continuum. The continuity is attested especially by the rejection of the traditional Christian concept of eternity, which is essentially Greek in origin, where eternity means timelessness, the denial of temporality. Mormonism conceives of God as being in both time and space. The natural continuum is evidenced as well in the Mormon view that there is no immaterial substance and that spiritual entities are not less material than physical objects.

D + C

131 : 7

This naturalistic quality of Mormon philosophy is without question related to several facets of the attitude, practice, and thought of the Mormon people: the high evaluation placed on the human body, the essentially positive attitude toward sex, the affirmative estimate of human character and human accomplishment, the obvious this-worldliness of the religion with its denial of the distinction between the sacred and the secular, and a traditional enthusiasm for natural science. It is perhaps not entirely inaccurate to describe Mormonism as a kind of naturalistic, humanistic theism.

2. On Necessity and Contingency

BUT TO RETURN TO THE IDEA that the world is not created in the ultimate sense, the Mormon scripture *The Doctrine and Covenants* states the matter succinctly, "The elements are eternal. . . ."[1] This is taken by Mormon writers to mean that the basic constituents of which the world is composed are without beginning and without end and are therefore uncreated. More than that, Joseph Smith elsewhere advanced the idea that also among the uncreated, beginningless, and endless entities are human souls or spirits, which he referred to as minds or intelligences. It was clearly his view, and one accepted in the Mormon Church, that whatever is ultimate and essential in the human soul is self-existent. It is assumed in Mormon thought, moreover, that space and time are uncreated, as are certain objective "principles" in terms of which reality is structured.

Now among metaphysical problems, one of the most basic and interesting is the question of "necessary" and "contingent" being. By "necessary" being is meant the being of whatever could not *not* exist. Anything has contingent being if its being is not

necessary, that is if it could *not* exist. Whatever has contingent
being is contingent upon or dependent upon something else for its
existence. In traditional occidental theism, only God is described
as having original necessary being. All else is contingent. Indeed,
one of the classical arguments for God set forth by St.
Thomas Aquinas in his famous five proofs[2] is the argument that since the
objects of nature are obviously contingent, or what he calls "possible" only, there must be a necessary being to account for their
existence.

But in Mormonism, in the deepest reaches of his nature even
man has necessary being, a doctrine that has important implications for the Mormon religion. Man is necessary not in the sense
that his non-being would be a contradiction or that it is impossible
to conceive of his nonexistence or of the world existing without
him, but rather in the sense that his existence is a given fact of
the world, that nothing is more original than his ultimate being.
In traditional Christian doctrine man's reality is rooted in the
creative act of God. Where God is infinite, man therefore is
finite; where God is eternal, man is temporal; where God is secure,
man is ontologically insecure; and where God is identical with the
very fact of reality, the existence of man is inevitably in doubt and
precarious. In traditional Christian theology the primary sin of
man, the sin of pride, is his rebellion against his own contingency,
his denial of his finiteness, his setting himself thereby in opposition to God. Here he suffers alienation and estrangement, an
estrangement from the ground of his own being, out of which
issues the anguish of his soul, the anxieties of guilt, of meaninglessness, and death.

In principle at least, Mormonism is opposed to this description of the human predicament, the Mormon conception of man
having far more in common with typical modern religious liberalism or even humanism than with either secular or religious existentialism. For though in Mormon doctrine man is finite, the human
spirit has the foundation of its existence within itself, and whatever dependence man has on God — and his dependencies are

very great — it is yet believed that his temporality does not separate him from God and that utter contingency is not the condition of his being, for he is not totally God's creature. More than anything else it is this belief, that man though finite nevertheless has necessary being, that constitutes the philosophical justification of much of the substance of Mormon theology which stands in opposition to the classical Christian orthodoxy.

3. On Materialism

AN INTERESTING AND IMPORTANT FACET of the Mormon conception of reality is the materialism that is defended so consistently and emphatically by Mormon writers. From very early times materialism has been found in both oriental and occidental thought, but its appearance within the framework of theistic philosophy is quite uncommon. The Greek atomists and the Hellenistic and Roman Epicureans were materialistic in their theories of reality, but all of these were in principle opposed to theistic religion. In recent centuries materialism has usually opposed religion. This is true to a considerable extent of the materialism of the French Enlightenment in the eighteenth century and also the materialism of nineteenth-century German philosophy, including the somewhat atypical materialism of Marxism. Roman Stoicism is perhaps the major instance of a materialistic philosophy with religious inclinations, but Stoicism's materialism was combined with a quite thoroughgoing monism and in its religious form it was essentially pantheistic rather than theistic.

The anti-religious tendency of materialism is associated especially with the mechanistic character of typical materialism, where there seems to be a denial of every kind of freedom in favor of a strict causal determinism. In such a system there is no contingency and every event occurs necessarily; that is, it could not have not occurred. The Epicureans attempted to avoid the deterministic implications of their materialism, but the Greek atomists and Stoics were frankly deterministic, as was the seven-

teenth-century Englishman Thomas Hobbes, the foremost of the
modern materialists. It is especially in the denial of determinism
in its commitment to a libertarian doctrine of the freedom of the
will that Mormonism differs from the usual form of materialism,
a difference that is important for both morals and religion.

The materialism of Mormonism is not in any way a denial
of the reality of the spirit or of heavenly beings. Mormonism
teaches a strict numerical dualism of the spirit and body; though
they are both material, they are two different entities. But the
dualism is in number or degree only and not in the fundamental
quality or character of reality, a fact which distinguishes the
Mormon position from the typical mind-body dualism that has
typified Protestant thought, for instance, since Descartes. Mormon
writers have commonly taken the position of typical materialism,
that in principle the only reality is matter in motion in space and
time. Indeed, they have sometimes held that the very concept
of an immaterial substance, a concept of immense importance in
traditional philosophic and religious thought, is a logical contradiction, a view also held by Hobbes. The case for materialism is
stated explicitly in *The Doctrine and Covenants*: "There is no
such thing as immaterial matter. All spirit is matter, but it is more
fine or pure, and can only be discerned by purer eyes; We cannot
see it . . . ."[3]

The Mormon-type materialism is not unknown within the
confines of Christian theology, but it is most uncommon and is
regarded as a radical heresy by both Catholicism and Protestantism. The most celebrated early theologian to advocate this type
of materialism was the third-century Roman, Tertullian, a vigorous opponent of the Gnostic form of Christianity which held
matter to be evil and the source of evil. In his *De Anima*, Tertullian described the soul as corporeal. His essay on the soul is in
part a polemic against Plato, who was the main source of the
Christian doctrine of the immateriality of the soul, but he agreed
with Plato that the soul is simple rather than compound. The
Mormon view, agreeing with Tertullian's materialism and with

But were we not begotten spiritually?

Plato's belief in the preexistence and uncreatedness of the soul, disagrees with both in holding that the spirit is a compound of elements.

It is typical of a materialistic metaphysics, as for instance that of the pre-Socratic atomistic philosopher Democritus, to hold that matter is essentially lifeless and inert and that the motions of matter are due to external mechanical forces. An effort has been made by some Mormon theologians, especially the pioneer apostle Orson Pratt, to develop a theory of matter as in some sense living and intelligent. Pratt's views, which do not enjoy official acceptance by the Church, amount to a kind of panpsychism reminiscent of the monadology of the seventeenth-century German mathematician and philosopher Leibniz, who held that all reality consists of mind atoms that are living centers of force. At any rate the Mormon concept of matter is that it is essentially dynamic rather than static, if indeed it is not a kind of living energy, and that it is subject at least to the rule of intelligence.

It is important to recognize that the mind-body problem, the question of the nature of the soul or spirit and the body and the relation between them, has been a major metaphysical issue in occidental religious thought since the earliest Christian centuries. The Mormon treatment of this problem, which is radically unorthodox when judged by either Catholic or Protestant thought, nevertheless conforms to the general pattern of Christian theology, that the soul or spirit is immortal though the body is subject to death. In at least one interesting and not unimportant feature the Mormon doctrine has some similarities to Catholicism in this matter. Whereas Protestantism has quite commonly followed the Cartesian conception of a radical difference between mind and body, where they are described as so totally different in character that it is difficult to account for their connection, Catholicism, following St. Thomas Aquinas, has emphasized their integral relationship by describing the soul as the form of the body. This theory is supported by subtle metaphysical arguments drawn from Aristotle, and I do not mean to suggest that Mormonism holds the same view. But the tendency of Mormonism is, never-theless, in the somewhat similar direction of describing the soul and the body in terms that tend to relate them to one another rather than to separate them by the radical difference in their natures.

4. On Monism and Pluralism

ONE OF THE MOST INTERESTING problems in metaphysics centers in the question whether reality is one or many. This issue can be approached in terms of quality, whether there is more than one *kind* of reality, or in terms of quantity, whether reality is single or is a plurality of entities. For Mormonism, as has already been shown, reality conceived qualitatively is in a sense dualistic but in another sense monistic. There are two kinds of reality, mind and matter, but they are different only in degree and not in nature and are both describable, therefore, by the same categories.

If we turn from the question of the kinds of reality to the question of quantity, the position of Mormonism is immediately evident — a thoroughgoing pluralism. It is taken for granted that the world is a collection of individual entities that are real taken in their individuality, whether they are things, processes, or events. There is no all-inclusive, single reality that is the being of all the others, in which they are in some way inherent, of which they are facets, expressions, or aspects. The world is genuinely additive in the sense that, theoretically, additions to it or subtractions from it could be made without disturbing the totality of reality, for that totality is a collection rather than a single absolute. The world is a multiverse rather than a universe.

The pluralistic character of the Mormon view of reality can be seen at many levels: the tendency to think of the spirit as a com-pound of entities rather than as simple, in itself a major departure from classical Christian metaphysics; the clear conception that in its original nature the world is composed of independently real intelligences and material elements; the rigorous distinction between man and God or God and the world; or the tritheistic conception of the Godhead, where the Father, Son, and Holy Ghost are described as three ontologically separate beings. Of course all theistic philosophy, as in Judaism, Islam, and Christianity, is somewhat pluralistic in character, for the failure to distinguish at least between God and his creations is pantheism, a position commonly regarded as heretical by the established religions. It is especially the biblical origin of living occidental religions that guarantees their opposition to pantheism, for the Bible clearly militates against the identification of God with the world of his creation. In theism God is conceived as in a sense immanent in the world, but as also transcendent to it. The Christian theologies have inclined in various directions, Lutheranism toward immanence, for instance, and Calvinism toward transcendence; but for the most part a balance of the two has been maintained. Mormonism, which in most respects has more in common with Calvinism than with Lutheranism, is very pronounced in its transcendentalism, though its conception of the Holy Spirit entails some measure of immanentism.

Though the metaphysics of the established Christianity is not monistic, it commonly exhibits a less strenuous pluralism than is found in Mormonism and has strong absolutistic tendencies though always falling short of a genuine absolutism. These tendencies can be seen especially in the traditional descriptions of the nature of God, from which Mormonism is a radical departure, and they have a strong support in the ancient doctrine of the *ex nihilo* creation, a doctrine which is emphatically denied by Mormonism.

The tension between monism and pluralism in metaphysics has been a major fact of the history of occidental philosophy. Thus among the ancient Greeks, Parmenides was a monist, Democritus a pluralist, and Plato somewhere in between. Aristotle was a pluralist and the great Roman Platonist, Plotinus, was something of a monist. The pluralistic character of Catholicism is protected in part by the large Aristotelian element in the metaphysics of St. Thomas Aquinas. Of modern philosophers, Spinoza was an intense monist and absolutist, Leibniz a pluralist, Hegel an absolutist and essentially therefore a monist, and William James a pluralist. James, whose pluralism reflects much of the character of typical American thought, was the most brilliant of all the polemicists against absolutism and monism. Many of his views are remarkably similar to the ideas characteristic of Mormonism, a fact in which he himself took considerable interest. The most celebrated monist among American philosophers was James's colleague at Harvard, Josiah Royce. But even Royce's absolutism reflected the typical American penchant for pluralism in its effort to provide for the reality of individual selves within the structure of the Absolute.

The relation of metaphysics to the ways of knowing is of basic importance in the construction and justification of a theory of reality. There are three basic methods by which knowledge claims are established: reason, intuition, and experience, where experience usually means sensory experience. Knowledge by revelation is usually described as a form of intuition, a term intended to refer to the claim that knowledge can be obtained by an immediate direct involvement of the knowing subject with the object of knowledge.

This is an intricate and lengthy subject and cannot be exploited here, but it should be observed that those who incline toward empiricism, the view that knowledge must eventually derive from sensory experience, usually also favor a pluralistic metaphysics, for the world appears to the senses as a multiplicity of individual objects in space and events in time. Those who favor a rationalistic method, in its classical form the presumed rational deduction of propositions from initial premises that are known to be true independently of experience — as in the old axiomatic conception of geometry — often incline toward a monistic or absolutistic metaphysics. Their monism follows from the fact that, in the first place, they declare a considerable measure of independence from the dictates of sensory experience, freeing themselves from pluralistic presuppositions; in the second place they find the world to be a logically coherent unity that matches the logical order of their reasoning processes. Intuition, when it is mystical in character, also tends to yield a monistic or absolutistic metaphysics, because in typical reports of the mystic experience the subject experiences a union with the object, or at least a deep sense of the unity of the world.

Now there is not in Mormonism anything like an officially accepted position on the methodology of knowledge, beyond the acceptance of the principle of revelation. Indeed, there is not an official technical definition or description of the nature of revelation. It is not possible, therefore, to describe for Mormonism the relation of the ways of knowing to the nature of reality with anything like an explicit thesis. But it is possible to say that Mormonism in its philosophical inclinations participates strongly in the empirical attitudes that are characteristic of recent and contemporary thought. It acknowledges the claims of scientific method — a combination of empiricism and qualified rationalism — and it even exhibits sensory empirical leanings in its references to revelation. It can at least be said that a common-sense empiricism seems to be not unrelated to the explicit pluralism of Mormon metaphysics.

5. On Being and Becoming

ANOTHER IMPORTANT AND INTERESTING issue in metaphysics is whether reality is static and changeless or dynamic and in process, a distinction that is commonly made by the terms "being" and "becoming." Among the ancient Greek philosophers, for instance, Heraclitus argued for a metaphysic of becoming, insisting that reality is characterized by process and change. "Everything," he said, "is on the move." That only is changeless which is the principle or law of orderly change, the Logos, which can be known by the reason but not by the senses. Whatever can be sensed, the world of existing things, can be apprehended only in its changing states, for there is not as much as a substratum that is not in constant flow and movement. For a metaphysic of being, on the other hand, there is no better example than that of Parmenides of Elea, one of the foremost minds of antiquity, who held that reality is one and is absolutely without motion, change, or process. Parmenides was, of course, a thoroughgoing rationalist who held that knowledge is essentially an affair of reason and logic and is not obtained through sensory impressions. Our senses, therefore, in revealing to us an objective world that is dynamic and unstable, are deceiving us. Reason, he insisted, gives us a world of genuine being, a world changeless, motionless, and absolute. Plato, who was greatly influenced by Parmenides, held that there are two orders of reality — a pluralistic world of particular objects existing in space and time, changing, growing, and decaying, known to us through our sense perceptions; and a world of immutable reality, static and timeless, where unity is more ultimate than plurality, a world of universals rather than particulars, a reality known not by sense experience but by the processes of abstract thought and intuition.

It is important to see that when reality is described as absolute, static, and changeless it is also regarded as timeless, and if it is described as dynamic and moving, it is held to be temporal. This is because time and motion must be defined by reference to each other. There cannot be time without motion or motion without time. So Plato's immutable realities are timeless, or in the technical sense, "eternal," without succession of past, present, and future. Traditional Christian theology has been greatly influenced by Platonism and commonly distinguishes two orders of reality, the timeless or eternal order of divinity, and the temporal order of God's creation, the world and mankind.

Now from its beginning Mormonism has laid much stress on the dynamic character of reality. This is evident in many connections, as in the occasional tendency to think of matter as being in some way active rather than entirely inert, or in the intense emphasis on freedom of choice and action in opposition to determinism. Nowhere, however, is the Mormon metaphysic of becoming more in evidence than in the idea that God himself is a temporal being with a past, present, and future, a being genuinely involved in the processes of the world. This doctrine is in certain respects a radical departure from classical Christian theology and its implications are far-reaching and profound for Mormonism. The common Mormon idea that man participates with God in an endless and progressive creative process is dependent upon the concept of the temporality of God. And nothing looms larger in Mormon thought or has more practical implications than this belief in what the Mormons usually call "eternal progress." The foremost of the accepted Mormon theologians, the historian Brigham H. Roberts, has employed the term "eternalism" as a description of Mormon philosophy, using the word "eternal" not in its technical meaning of timelessness, as it is most often employed in Christian theology, but rather as meaning unbegun and endless time. It would be quite impossible to grasp the character of Mormonism without recognizing that Mormon thought is oriented to a grand conception of cosmic process in an infinite time and space in which human freedom plays a fundamental and crucial role.

6. On Universals and Particulars

A FINAL PROBLEM that deserves some attention is the question whether in the Mormon theory of reality, where such great emphasis is placed on process, there is anything that is genuinely stable and unchanging. It would be a most exceptional religion that did not have some absolutes, and such absolutes are not difficult to locate in Mormonism. Certainly the moral will of God, or what might be called the divine purpose, is such an absolute, and notwithstanding their obvious practicalism, the Mormons are fully committed to value absolutes. In such matters they quite clearly reflect their Puritan ancestry. They assume, moreover, that the natural processes of the world are orderly rather than chaotic and that therefore the laws governing those processes are at least stable if not absolute. In brief, there is a cosmic order that embraces both the material structure and the value structure of the universe. It is typical of the Mormons to believe in an objective moral order as well as an objective order of the physical world.

Though on the surface this does not appear to be different from any typical theistic religion and philosophy, there is in fact a difference, and a most important difference. The historical sources of the Christian position on such matters are, of course, very complex, but the chief factor in the picture is the Greek concept of universals as set forth in Platonism, the most influential philosophy of antiquity. The nature of a universal is most readily understood by comparing it with a particular. A particular in metaphysics is any particular thing or event. It has existence in space and time — it is somewhere and at some time. A white object, a human being, or an act of justice is a particular. Universals can be identified as the attributes of particulars, treated as nouns rather than as adjectives. So just as a white object is a particular, whiteness is a universal. A human being is a particular, but humanity is a universal. And a just act is a particular, but justice is a universal. A true proposition is a particular, but truth is a universal. A good act is a particular, but goodness is a universal, and so forth.

Now there is no metaphysical problem of greater importance than the question of whether universals are in some sense real entities rather than simply words employed to call attention to similarities that obtain among particulars. Do truth and justice, for instance, have some kind of objective reality, or are they just words employed to describe sentences and acts? Plato's most important idea, and perhaps the most important of all philosophic ideas, was that universals do have an objective status in the structure of being. They have, he held, an independent existence, and the nature of particulars is determined by their participation in the universals, or what he called *Ideas* with a capital "I." Truth is real and eternal. Justice is real and eternal. Goodness is real and eternal — eternal in the sense of being timeless and immutable.

But in Platonism there is no living, personal God. The Platonic universals are not attributes of God. They are impersonal absolutes that are the foundation structure of the universe — uncreated, unchanging, and indestructible.

Now to make a very long and difficult story very short and simple, the juncture of early biblical Christian theology with Greek metaphysics within the Hellenistic culture of the Graeco-Roman world brought the impersonal, eternal, Platonic universals into conjunction with the living, personal God of the Hebrew Bible as descriptions of the highest or most ultimate reality or being. The essential outcome — as found for instance in the fourth-century theory of St. Augustine, the most influential of the Christian theologians — was the description of the biblical God in terms of the Greek universals. Much of the history of Christian doctrine is summarized in this development. Truth is real and eternal; beauty is real and eternal; and justice is real and eternal, because truth, beauty, and justice are real absolutes in the mind of the living God. They and the multitude of other absolutes determine the divine will and provide the structure of the universe. Sometimes, as in a prolonged medieval controversy between the intellectualistically inclined Dominicans and the voluntaristic Franciscans, the question of the priority of God's will over his intellect or his intellect over his will was at issue, but it was rarely a question of God's will or intellect being subject to anything external to the divine nature.

But to return to Mormonism and a most important aspect of its philosophy. Mormonism has not developed a theory of universals, or anything like an explicit position on that subject. There is abundant evidence, nevertheless, that the reality of universals is taken for granted in typical Mormon theology, and not only value universals, which give the universe its moral texture and provide absolutistic foundations for the moral law, but also a host of other universals which provide the world with its cosmic structure. Mormon writers often use such words as "laws" or "principles" to indicate such universals. But the point is — and it is a decisive one — that at least some of the universals are commonly regarded as existing independently of God, their status being remarkably like that assigned to them by early Platonism — impersonal absolutes that are the foundation of reality. Indeed, some Mormon theologians even account for God's status in terms of his relationship to the universals, where in his divinity he is in a sense subject to them rather than they subject to him. This idea appears in extreme form in the writings of the Mormon apostle Orson Pratt, though it cannot be regarded as conforming to Mormon orthodoxy because it appears to deny that, in the last analysis, God as God is a person. In 1853 Pratt wrote:

> Persons are only tabernacles or temples, and TRUTH is the God, that dwells in them. If the fullness of truth, dwells in numberless millions of persons, then the same one indivisible God dwells in them all. . . . When we worship the Father, we do not merely worship His person, but we worship the truth which dwells in His person. . . . Wherever you find a fullness of wisdom, knowledge, truth, goodness, love, and such like qualities, there you find God in all His glory, power, and majesty, therefore, if you worship these adorable perfections you worship God.[4]

More familiar and more generally accepted universals can be seen in the common Mormon conceptions of the *Church* and *Priesthood*. Here the Mormon position is not entirely unlike that of Catholicism, which has a long history of involvement with the problem of universals and is highly sophisticated in philosophical matters of this kind. It is common for Mormons to distinguish individual Church members, for instance, from the *Church*, where the Church is not only not identified simply with its members but also is not exhausted in its institutions. The *Church* seems to be a kind of reality that cannot be identified with any form of particularity. This is not to suggest that there is anything like an official Mormon doctrine that describes the Church as a universal, but simply that the Mormon people speak and write as if this were the case. In contrast, for instance, Protestantism, which in its early development was much influenced by the nominalistic metaphysics which denies the reality of universals, has often conceived the Church essentially as the congregation of the believers in Christ.

A better example, perhaps, is the Mormon conception of the Priesthood, for here there is something like a clear-cut orthodox position favoring the idea that the Priesthood is a universal. It would be impossible for a Mormon, for instance, or a Catholic, to say that there are as many priesthoods as there are priests. The Mormons clearly regard the Priesthood as a real universal entity that does not have its reality grounded in particular priests. Rather they are priests by virtue of a possession of the Priesthood. A statement from Joseph Smith quite clearly indicates that the term "priesthood" is not simply a collective term, but is intended to refer to some kind of universal reality: "The Priesthood is an everlasting principle, and existed with God from eternity, and will to eternity, without beginning of days or end of years."[5]

On the other hand, there are evidences in Mormonism of rather strong tendencies in the direction of nominalism, the view that only particulars are real, particular events or objects, and that so-called universals are but names, or at best useful concepts. There is a strong tendency in Mormon thought to incline away from abstractions and toward the particular and concrete, a posture that commonly yields a nominalistic metaphysics. The Mormon conception of the Godhead, for instance, is tritheistic rather than trinitarian, the Mormon scriptures and theologians explicitly advancing and defending the idea that the Father, Son, and Holy Ghost are three separate and distinct beings. The Mormon theology rejects the Nicene doctrine that has been normative for Catholicism since the fourth century, and for most Protestants, that the three are one in substance. Their unity, in the Mormon view, is a unity of will, a perfect harmony of purpose, but not the unity of identity in their essential being. In the history of Christianity the heresy of tritheism has sometimes been associated with nominalism, as in the case of the condemnation by

the Council of Soisson in 1092 of the celebrated nominalist Ros-
cellinus on the ground that his metaphysics entailed a tritheistic
denial of the trinity.

It would be an error to suppose that Mormon theological
doctrine is a deduction from metaphysical principles. Certainly
nothing could be further from the truth. Mormonism is basically
a dogmatic religion grounded in the claims of revelation. But it
is clear that the Mormon theology has a foundation in a set of
ideas on the nature of things and that some acquaintance with
those ideas is essential to an understanding of the conceptions of
God and man which are central to the religion of the Mormon
people. Although historically the theology was not derived logically from the metaphysics, the metaphysics is logically prior to
the theology.

PART TWO

THE CONCEPT OF GOD

7. On Creation

AN UNDERSTANDING OF THE MORMON conceptions of God and man requires some insight into the Mormon view on the matter of creation, for here is an important ground of the difference that obtains between Mormonism and the classical theology. Mormonism denies the traditional doctrine of creation *ex nihilo* and this denial supports its finitistic theology and its radically unorthodox doctrine of man. The general format of classical Christian theology was established at Alexandria in the first century by Philo Judaeus, the foremost Jewish philosopher of antiquity, who attempted a reconciliation of the dominant Hellenistic metaphysics of his time with the Hebrew scriptures. Philo rejected the Aristotelian concept of the world as uncreated, especially on the ground, apparently, that such a theory is incompatible with Aristotle's own view of God as active cause. The belief that the world is uncreated, he held, is impious as well as erroneous and it casts doubt on the reality of providence. And though he accepted the Platonic theory, advanced especially in the *Timaeus*, that the world is fashioned by God from preexistent matter, Philo insisted on the questionable interpretation of Plato that both the matter and the *Ideas*, or forms, according to which the world was structured, were creations of God, creations from

nothing. Contrary to the Stoics, who held to the inevitable destruction of the world, Philo accepted its destructibility as a consequence of its being created, but argued that God will guarantee
it from destruction.

Although Justin,[1] Origen of Alexandria,[2] and others of the
early Christian fathers, finding support in Plato and in certain
Hebrew writings, rejected the doctrine of creationism, by the
end of the second century the *ex nihilo* doctrine was accepted
almost universally in the Church, its acceptance being in part a
consequence of the controversy with Gnosticism as well as the
influence of the Philonic school. Creationism became widely
accepted also in Jewish philosophy.[3]

The *ex nihilo* doctrine is a fundamental of Catholic theology,
where it is held, as by Philo, to be scriptural. In the *Summa
Theologica*, for instance, St. Thomas Aquinas, who, in conformity
to the general Christian tradition, vigorously opposed the common
Greek idea that matter is uncreated, held that ". . . everything,
that in any way is, is from God. . . . God is self-subsisting being
itself . . . all beings other than God are not their own being, but
are beings by participation."[4] He added, "Nothing except God
can be eternal . . . [for] . . . the will of God is the cause of things."[5]
That the world did not always exist is indemonstrable and must
therefore be held, according to Aquinas, as an article of faith.[6]

That the world was created by a divine fiat had already been
brilliantly argued by St. Augustine in the Eleventh Book of *The
Confessions*.

> But how didst Thou make the heaven and the earth, and
> what was the instrument of Thy so mighty work? For it
> was not as a human worker fashioning body from body,
> according to the fancy of his mind, in somewise able to
> assign a form which it perceives in itself by its inner eye.
> . . . And he assigns to it already existing, and as it were
> having a being, a form, as clay, or stone, or wood, or gold,
> or such like. . . . How, O God, didst Thou make heaven
> and earth? Truly, neither in the heaven nor in the earth
> didst Thou make heaven and earth; nor in the air, nor in

the waters, since these also belong to the heaven and the
earth; nor in the whole world didst Thou make the whole
world, because there was no place wherein it could be made
before it was made, that it might be; nor didst Thou hold
anything in Thy hand wherewith to make heaven and
earth. For whence couldest Thou have what Thou hadst
not made, whereof to make anything? For what is, save
because Thou art? Therefore Thou didst speak and they
were made, and in Thy Word Thou madest these things.[7]

The Swiss theologian Karl Barth has restated the Augustinian
position for contemporary Protestant neoorthodoxy, a position
which is characteristic of traditional Protestantism. "Creaturely
reality means reality on the basis of a *creatio ex nihilo*, a creation
out of nothing. Where nothing exists — and not a kind of primal
matter — there through God there has come into existence that
which is distinct from Him. . . . Everything outside God is held
constant by God over nothingness. Creaturely nature means
existence in time and space, existence with a beginning and an
end, existence that becomes, in order to pass away again. Once it
was not, and once it will no longer be."[8]

The *ex nihilo* or *fiat* account of the world's origin commonly
includes the idea that the human spirit or soul or ego is a product
of God's creative act and denies the possibility of any preexistence
of the soul. (The term "soul" is employed here, as in typical usage,
as synonymous with "spirit." In Mormon terminology the two
are distinguished.) Beyond the denial of preexistence, however,
there has been considerable controversy in Christian theology on
the beginnings of the soul, as especially between *traducianism*,
which holds that individual souls are descended by generation
from the soul of Adam, and *creationism*, that each individual soul
is the product of a special and immediate creative act of God at
conception or birth. Tertullian and, for a time, Augustine advo-
cated traducianism as a means of explaining original sin, but
creationism is the established doctrine of Catholicism. St. Thomas
Aquinas, whose theology is today normative for Roman Catholi-

cism, rejected traducianism as heretical,[9] and also declared against the doctrine that "human souls were created together at the beginning of the world."[10] However, due especially to its usefulness in accounting for the transmission of original sin as a depravity of the soul, traducianism has had considerable acceptance in Protestantism, especially Calvinism.

It should be recognized, of course, that the concept of creation has been interpreted variously and at times has been entirely abandoned in theistic philosophy. Indeed, in the tradition of liberal Protestantism it has been a center of major dispute, not simply as a subject in cosmological speculation but because the entire problem is central to the discussion of the nature of man and his predicament. Friedrich Schleiermacher, for instance, who was certainly one of the chief determiners of the course of liberal theology, exhibited mystical and idealistic tendencies which counted against the transcendentalism of the classical doctrine of creation in favor of an immanentism that, while not identifying God and the world, at least treated them as correlates such as "right" and "left." Although he was not a genuine pantheist, Schleiermacher flirted somewhat blatantly with pantheism, holding with Spinoza, for instance, that God does not create freely and that for him possibility and actuality cannot be distinguished. Certainly for Schleiermacher, as for liberal theologians generally, the doctrine of the *ex nihilo* creation made little sense, at least in its traditional form.

This does not mean, however, that it has been entirely abandoned by liberal theology. Frederick R. Tennant, whose *Philosophical Theology* is the most impressively reasoned modern argument for theism, while admitting its inadvisability as explanation, defends the concept of creation on the ground that it is a valid ultimate assumption.

> The *modus operandi* of divine creativity is wholly unimaginable and inconceivable. And this inexplicability is inevitable. For explanation, in all its forms, establishes some connexion, similarity, or continuity, with what is

experienced or lies within Experience; whereas creation is
the activity through which experients and what is experienced by them come to be. The notion of creation, consequently, is not derivable from experience, and analogies
valid within experience cannot reach beyond its bounds.
But while the theist must confess that a conception which
is fundamental in his philosophy is inexplicable, he may do
so without shame and without reproach. Some ultimates,
unanalysable and unassimilable, there must be. Theism
needs but allow that creation is one of them.[11]

The defense of creation is found even among the metaphysical
idealists, but here the concept is not ordinarily employed, as in
orthodoxy and neoorthodoxy, as a device for accentuating the
total disparity of the divine and human natures. This is especially
evident in personalistic idealism, that form of idealism which has
effected the greatest impact on recent liberal Protestantism, as
evidenced, for instance, in the work of the German Hegelian,
Hermann Lotze, and the American, Borden Parker Bowne. Lotze
defended the concept of creation but specifically denied that there
is or has been a "process" of creation. "The conception of creation
properly signifies nothing more than this; that the world, with
respect to its existence as well as its content, is completely dependent upon the will of God, and not a mere involuntary 'development' of his nature; that it proceeds, however, only from the
will and not from a special work of God. . . ."[12]

Bowne, who was importantly influenced by Lotze and who in
turn exerted a powerful impact on early twentieth-century American Protestant thought, both churched and unchurched, also
denied creation as a temporal process but defended the notion of
"eternal" creation. "Many theologians," said Bowne approvingly,
"have declared for an eternal creation, and have further declared
creation to mean not temporal origination, but simply and only
the dependence of the world on God."[13] Whether this concept
of "eternal" as opposed to "temporal" creation can be invested
with genuine meaning is a question that both Lotze and Bowne
failed to adequately examine.

In opposition to the *ex nihilo* doctrine, especially as it relates to
the problem of evil, the distinguished Swedish-American idealist,
John Elof Boodin, argued for an unorthodox conception of creation that is essentially Platonic in character and not entirely unlike
the accepted view in Mormon theology. "We must rid the scholastic tradition of its *a priori* excrescence of creation out of nothing.
God is present everywhere and always, as creative spirit giving
form to our world, but matter does not as mere primitive matter
derive from God, though it owes its structure to God."[14] Though
his metaphysics was oriented in a profound understanding of
modern physical science, Boodin expressed himself in essentially
poetic terms. "I deem it a divine inspiration," he said, "that a
mighty spirit broods benignantly over chaos and that creation is
the child. . . . Creation is the reclaiming, the moulding, the persuasion of chaos into forms of beauty."[15]

A final exhibit: the British-American philosopher, Alfred
North Whitehead, perhaps the foremost speculative mind of the
past half-century, who quite like Boodin denied the traditional
conception of creation. God, wrote Whitehead, in his discussion
of the "consequent" nature of God in his Gifford Lectures, "does
not create the world, he saves it: or, more accurately, he is the
poet of the world, with tender patience leading it by his vision
of truth, beauty, and goodness."[16] Whitehead and Boodin were
both preoccupied with the fact of tragedy when they made their
attempt upon the problem of God's relation to the world, a fact
that appears to account for the somewhat poetic quality of their
metaphysics even though both were rigorously grounded in the
sciences.

The established Mormon doctrine is squarely opposed to the
traditional concept of creation and is in principle reminiscent
of the position common to the classical Greek naturalism. That
position, which denies creation as an original beginning, was clearly
enunciated in the fifth century before Christ by Parmenides of
Elea. Parmenides, who identified *being* with that which it is possible to think, insisted that *not being* does not exist because it is not

thinkable. Therefore there can be no coming into *being* from not-being. "How could Being perish? How could it come into being? If it came into being, it Is Not; and so too if it is about-to-be at some future time. Thus Coming-into-Being is quenched, and Destruction also into the unseen."[17]

As indicated earlier, the Mormon scripture *The Doctrine and Covenants* asserts simply that "The elements are eternal. . . ."[18] The term "eternal" here is commonly taken to mean unbegun and endless time rather than a state of timelessness in the sense of non-temporality. Elsewhere Joseph Smith argued that the classical doctrine of creation is an error, that "God had materials to organize the world out of chaos — chaotic matter, which is element. . . . Element had an existence from the time He [God] had."[19]

It is common for Mormon writers, in defense of their position on creation, to deny that the traditional doctrine of creation is biblical, a denial not uncommon in Protestant biblical scholarship. Brigham H. Roberts argued, for instance, that " 'Beginnings' and 'endings' for New Dispensation thought have reference to local events within the universe. . . . The opening verse of the *Bible* for instance — 'In the beginning God created the heaven and the earth' — has no reference to any 'absolute beginning' or creation from 'nothing,' but refers to the 'beginning' connected with our earth and the order of worlds with which it is connected."[20]

It is of interest that Mormonism holds a double-creation doctrine that is reminiscent of Philo, who argued that the two accounts of the creation set forth in Genesis (Chapters 1 and 2), which are often taken by modern scholarship as evidence of a compound documentary structure of Genesis, are accounts of a first creation of the Platonic ideas or universals, the "intelligible" world, and a second creation of the world of material particulars which exemplify those universals. In Mormon theology the first creation is a spiritual creation, where everything is created as spirit, and the second is the material creation which is a counterpart of the spiritual. In Philo the relationship between the creations is ontological but probably not chronological, while in the Mormon conception the second seems to follow temporally after the first. The Mormon double-creation doctrine is based especially on a passage in the Mormon scripture *The Pearl of Great Price*: "For I, the Lord God, created all things, of which I have spoken, spiritually, before they were naturally upon the face of the earth."[21] Mormon writers have usually referred the "spiritual" and "natural" creations to the two Genesis accounts.

But it should not be forgotten that these "creations" are not from nothing. They are a fashioning of the world from preexistent, eternal, and indestructible elements that are given constituents of the universe having in themselves the ground of their own being. The created world can come into being and theoretically it can go out of being, for its existence is contingent upon God's creative act. But the elements which compose it, and, in typical Mormon thought, the space and time which they are in, cannot begin and cannot cease to exist, for they are "eternal" and have necessary being. And among these uncreated entities are the intelligences that are the essential being of persons, whether human or divine.

8. On God as Absolute or Finite

IN ITS CONCEPTION OF GOD as in its doctrine of man, Mormonism is a radical departure from the established theology, both Catholic and Protestant. But that departure is not primarily at the point of the personalistic and anthropomorphic description of God, as has been so commonly supposed. For all traditional Christian theology, being rooted in the Hebrew scriptures, is basically in some degree anthropomorphic, and that God is a person is a belief common to all Christians. Indeed, the biblical faith in a living, personal God is common to all the living occidental religions: Judaism, Christianity, and Islam. And although materialistic concepts dominate Mormon metaphysics and theology, something quite uncommon for Christian theism, the important distinction of the Mormon doctrine also does not reside simply in its materialism. That distinction is found, rather, in the finitism in the concept of God that follows necessarily from the denial of ultimate creation, a finitism that places Mormonism in fundamental opposition to the absolutism that has been a primary assumption of theological discussion throughout the history of Christian thought.

The Christian absolutism had its beginnings in part in the political orientation of the biblical concept of God and in the early rabbinical doctrine of God's moral sovereignty. But its philosophical rationalizations are derivatives of the classical Greek metaphysics that quite inevitably entered into both the substance and structure of Christian theology as a consequence of the development of Hellenistic Christianity as a confluence of Hebrew religion, Greek scientific and philosophic culture, and Roman legal and civic institutions. Platonic and Aristotelian metaphysics, mediated to Christianity especially through the Alexandrian philosopher Philo and by the religious forms of Stoicism and Neoplatonism, brought to the biblical personal God of primitive Christianity absolutistic descriptions that had been fashioned in the discussion of ultimate reality in the impersonalistic context of Greek thought. It is this anomalous predicament, as seen for instance in the greatest of the dogmatic theologians, St. Augustine, that has set for Christian thought its most persistent theological problems — problems issuing from the conjunction of Hebrew voluntarism and Greek rationalism, Hebrew supernaturalism and Greek naturalism, and especially Hebrew personalistic and temporalistic theism and Greek impersonalistic and non-temporalistic metaphysics.

In its technical meaning, the absolute is the unrelated and unconditioned. An absolutistic theology in the full sense of the word would be a form of pantheism which identified God with the whole of reality and where all possible relations and conditions would be internal to God, there being nothing external to him which could be a condition upon him. The tendency of Christian theology has been to press in the direction of absolutism while

attempting to avoid the extreme of pantheism. Its absolutistic
bias is reflected especially in its efforts to guarantee to God's nature
the traditional "omni's" — omniscience, omnipotence, and omnipresence. But this, of course, has at times involved it in paradox
or inconsistency, because genuine absolutism is in principle irrecon-
cilable with biblical theistic religion. Religious theism commonly
assumes God to be both immanent and transcendent, in the world
and yet other than the world, and it cultivates the mystic experience of the presence of God while denying the individual's identification with him.

Although theological absolutism runs the obvious risk of pantheism — the identification of God with whatever is real — pantheism has always been a Christian heresy, as it denies the obvious
teaching of the Judaeo-Christian scriptures that, however much
he may be involved with the world and in the world, God is
different from the world and is ontologically set over against it.
He is related to it as creator to creature. Nevertheless, Christian
theology has traditionally preferred the risk of pantheism to any
doctrine that might seriously threaten the presumed absoluteness
of the divine knowledge, power, and moral goodness. It has vigorously opposed every suggestion of a limitation on any one of these,
the opposition becoming especially strong with the threat of any
kind of dualism or pluralism in the conception of divine power.
The various forms of Gnosticism, for instance, that plagued Christianity in its earliest centuries with the distinction between the
creator God, who was responsible for the material evil world, and
the supreme God, the source of all goodness, were commonly condemned as heretical. And later St. Augustine, who was himself
a Manichee before his conversion, contended vigorously and suc-
cessfully against the Manichaean dualism that argued, on grounds
inherited from the ancient Persian Zoroastrianism, for the existence of a second god who is the champion of darkness and evil.
The devil, though prominent in Christian literature and legend,
has always been an embarrassment to sophisticated theology be-

cause as an explanation of evil his power would compromise the absoluteness of God.

The Mormon theologians have moved somewhat ambiguously between the emotionally satisfying absolutism of traditional theism and the radical finitism logically demanded by their denial of creation and encouraged by the pragmatic character of their daily faith. Here they have often failed to recognize the strength of their own position and have, therefore, neglected to grasp and appreciate the full meaning of its implications, a failure arising in part from their common commitment to biblical literalism and their attachment to the rhetorical forms of Christian orthodoxy, and in part also from their own brand of scholasticism and their often intense legalism.

When seen clearly and consistently, the concept of God that is characteristic of Mormon theology is consonant with and contributes to the pluralistic character of the Mormon conception of reality. God is described in non-absolutistic terms as a being who is conditioned by and related to the world of which he is a part and which, because it is not ultimately his creation, is not absolutely under his dominion. As a constructor or artisan God, not entirely unlike Plato's demiurge of the *Timaeus*, the Mormon deity informs the continuing processes of reality and determines the world's configurations, but he is not the creator of the most ultimate constituents of the world, either the fundamental material entities or the space and time that locate them. God's environment is the physical universe, the minds and selves which exist but are not identified with him, the principles under which reality is structured, and perhaps even the value absolutes which govern the divine will. In any case, it is entirely evident that it is a basic article of Mormon theology that God is related to a world environment for the being of which he is not the ultimate ground and by which he therefore is in some sense conditioned. This means that God is a being among beings rather than *being* as such or the ground of being, and that he is therefore finite rather than absolute.

Nothing in the history of Christian theology exhibits more subtlety or intellectual sophistication or has more far-reaching implications, both theoretical and practical, than the discussion of the "relative" absoluteness of God. For the question is not simply of God's relation to the material universe or to the souls or spirits of men, but also to space and time, and to such ideal realities as the values of truth, beauty, and goodness, or to the principles of logic and mathematics. When Christianity took its rise in the Graeco-Roman world, where its chief theological foundations were laid, there was already a long and respected metaphysical tradition that affirmed the reality, for instance, of the Platonic *Ideas* or universals, realities that compare with particular entities which exist in space and time as justice compares with just acts, humanity with human beings, or whiteness with white objects. The question of whether such entities have real being, and, if so, the nature of that being, is even today often regarded as the most basic issue in metaphysics. Any conception of God in a world in which the Platonic philosophy was a major intellectual factor, as it was in Graeco-Roman intellectual life, was inevitably confronted with the question of God's relation to the universals. Here again Philo, though a non-Christian Jew, was a major determinant of the beginnings of the Christian theology.

Affected by the absolutistic character of Platonic metaphysics as well as the transcendentalism of the post-exilic religion and the rabbinic theology, Philo described God in strongly absolutistic terms — as absolutistic, at least, as was compatible with the avoidance of pantheism and the maintenance of the distinction between God and the created world. "For the living God," he wrote, "inasmuch as he is living, does not consist in relation to anything; for he himself is full of himself, and he is sufficient for himself, and he existed before the creation of the world, and equally after the creation of the universe; for he is immovable and unchangeable, having no need of any other thing or being whatever, so that all things belong to him, but, properly speaking, he does not belong to anything."[22] Moreover, departing from

Plato's own position as set forth in the *Timaeus*, Philo made God the creator of the Platonic universals, thus guaranteeing that reality in its totality is either God or his creation. Not only the world that exists in space and time, but also the "intelligible" world which is its ideal pattern, is the creation of God.

In the fourth century, St. Augustine, who moved from Manichaeism to Christianity by way of Neoplatonism, attempted to solve the problem of the relation of the Christian God to the Platonic value universals not by regarding them as creations of God but rather by placing them in the divine mind as the objects of its eternal thought. He thereby secured their high reality and their dominion over the moral universe. Augustine's position in this matter is indicative of the manner in which Christian theology, especially Catholic, has preserved much of classical metaphysics while guaranteeing the ontological supremacy of the divine personality. What might otherwise have been God's environment has been either incorporated into his being, as in the instance of value universals, or made the product of his creative act, as for instance the material world and the souls of men, thus securing his nature, in a sense at least, as absolute — unrelated and unconditioned; not unrelated and unconditioned in the full and complete sense, but related to only that which the divine will itself has freely and purposefully created, and suffering only those conditions which are intentionally occasioned by that creation. But this quasi-absolutism, while solving several difficult theoretical problems and quite certainly satisfying many of the demands of practical religion, has generated numerous difficulties for theology with its constant threat of pantheism and its obvious implications for the problem of evil. Yet it is still supported by both Catholics and orthodox Protestants and, with some reservation, is defended more often than not even in the camp of the liberal religionists.

The *Dogmatic Decrees of the Vatican Council of 1870* clearly exhibit the absolutistic quality of the Catholic conception of God while at the same time distinguishing God from the created world and thereby avoiding pantheism.

> The holy Catholic Apostolic Roman Church believes and confesses that there is one true and living God, Creator and Lord of heaven and earth, almighty, eternal, immense, incomprehensible, infinite in intelligence, in will, and in all perfection, who, as being one, sole, absolutely simple and immutable spiritual substance, is to be declared as really and essentially distinct from the world, of supreme beatitude in and from himself, and ineffably exalted above all things which exist, or are conceivable, except himself.
>
> This one only true God, of his own goodness and almighty power, not for the increase or acquirement of his own happiness, but to manifest his perfection by the blessings which he bestows on creatures, and with absolute freedom of counsel, created out of nothing, from the very first beginning of time, both the spiritual and the corporeal creature, to wit, the angelical and the mundane, and afterwards the human creature, as partaking, in a sense, of both, consisting of spirit and of body.[23]

Classical Protestant theology, though essentially dogmatic rather than philosophical, retained the traditional absolutistic concept of God characteristic of Catholicism and defended it on the established orthodox assumptions and by the usual arguments. The intensive voluntarism which the Reformation derived especially from its attachments to Augustinianism resulted, in Calvinism at least, in an absolutism that was described less by the divine intellectual faculties, as in the scholastic philosophy against which the reformers had rebelled, and more by the total sovereignty of God's moral will. *The Westminster Confession of Faith, 1647,* the most important symbol arising from the impact of Calvinism in the British Isles, provides a most thorough description of God in absolutistic terms.

> There is but one only living and true God, who is infinite in being and perfection, a most pure spirit, invisible, without body, parts, or passions, immutable, immense, eternal, incomprehensible, almighty, most wise, most holy, most free, most absolute, working all things according to the counsel of his own immutable and most righteous will, for his own glory; most loving, gracious, merciful, long-suffer-

ing, abundant in goodness and truth, forgiving iniquity,
transgression, and sin. . . . God hath all life, glory, goodness,
blessedness, in and of himself; and is alone in and unto
himself all-sufficient, not standing in need of any creatures
which he hath made, nor deriving any glory from them,
but only manifesting his own glory in, by, unto, and upon
them: he is the alone foundation of all being, of whom,
through whom, and to whom are all things; and hath most
sovereign dominion over them, to do by them, for them,
or upon them whatsoever himself pleaseth. In his sight all
things are open and manifest; his knowledge is infinite,
infallible, and independent upon the creature; so as nothing is to him contingent or uncertain. He is most holy in all
his counsels, in all his works, and in all his commands.[24]

Perhaps the most impressive philosophic effort to justify the
absolutist description of God is the Gifford Lectures of the American philosopher Josiah Royce, who employed the most subtle devices of logic and metaphysics in an attempted reconciliation of
a genuine metaphysical absolutism with Christian theism, a reconciliation by which he hoped to avoid pantheism and preserve the
distinction between the divine self and human selves, a distinction
necessary to theistic religion and to the moral meaning of human
existence.

Whoever conceives the Absolute as a Self, conceives it
as in its form inclusive of an infinity of various, but inter-
woven and so of intercommunicating Selves, each one of
which represents the totality of the Absolute in its own
way, and with its own unity, so that the simplest con-
ceivable structure of the Absolute Life would be stateable
only in terms of an infinitely great variety of types of
purpose and of fulfillment, intertwined in the most complex fashions. Apart from any doctrine of evolution, then,
we have to regard the Absolute in its wholeness as com-
prising many Selves, in the most various interrelations.[25]

Tendencies toward finitistic theology in opposition to absolutism have occasionally appeared in modern religious thought, of
course, and they have to some extent been a mark of liberalism,

but the churches have quickly condemned them as heretical. The so-called empirical theologians of Great Britain, for instance, of whom Frederick R. Tennant in his *Philosophical Theology* is the most brilliant representative, cultivated finitistic concepts in conformity to their interest in moral experience as a foundation for constructive theology. And in the more-or-less free atmosphere of American thought, finitistic theology issued from the conjunction of nominalism and moralism in the pragmatic philosopher William James, who insisted that religious and philosophical ideas should conform to the dictates of common experience. Nowhere is the radical finitism of James more effectively expressed in contrast to traditional Christian absolutism than in his famous lines in *Pragmatism* when he said, in a statement that warms the heart of every Mormon reader:

> Suppose that the world's author put the case to you before creation, saying: "I am going to make a world not certain to be saved, a world the perfection of which shall be conditional merely, the condition being that each several agent does its own 'level best.' I offer you the chance of taking part in such a world. Its safety, you see, is unwarranted. It is a real adventure, with real danger, yet it may win through. It is a social scheme of co-operative work genuinely to be done. Will you join the procession? Will you trust yourself and trust the other agents enough to face the risk?" [26]

The finitism of James and his disciples enjoyed some acceptance in liberal Protestantism and in philosophically oriented theological discussion until the upsurge of the new orthodoxy in the decades of the 'thirties and 'forties. But today, with the decline of liberalism and the rise of irrationalism in religion, finitistic theology has lost much of its attractiveness. Although the Protestant liberalism that developed in various directions, especially in the nineteenth century, made radical departures from orthodoxy, particularly in overthrowing the dogma of original sin and the negative conception of man and in reconstructing the doctrine of Christ, and although in various ways they compromised its traditional forms, in general the liberals were reluctant to accept a finitistic conception of God. Notwithstanding its biblical criticism, its historical optimism, and its commitment to practical ends, the character of the liberal religion was, in some measure at least, the consequence of its widespread involvement both in Europe and America with the metaphysical absolutism of German Hegelianism and its philosophical heirs. Hegel's own immensely influential absolutistic metaphysics, whatever his pretensions, had little to do with Christianity; but the associations of Hegelianism with historical religious scholarship, the higher biblical criticism, and speculative ethics and theology, together with the enormous prestige of idealism as a world view, have guaranteed the perpetuity of absolutism even in unchurched philosophical theology. Even American personalistic idealism, with its strong emphasis on the individual, as in the work of Royce, Borden Parker Bowne, Ralph Tyler Flewelling, and Edgar S. Brightman, has generally perpetuated absolutism and encouraged the absolutistic conception of God in liberal theology. After all is said and done, it appears that those who seek the consolations and inspiration of religion are as a rule not willing to worship anything less than ultimate and absolute power. Clearly they are not willing to take their problems to a God who may have problems of his own. ha ha

Finitistic theology is not more popular among the Mormons than among others if they are judged by their typical sermons or rhetorical terminology. The word "finite" stirs nothing in the soul of the worshipper. But "infinite," "omnipotent," and "omniscient" are words made to order for the preacher and the popular writer. So Mormon theological writing and sermonizing are more often than not replete with the vocabulary of absolutism. But, like it or not, the Mormon theologian must sooner or later return to the finitistic conception of God upon which both his technical theology and his theological myths are founded. Here Mormonism reveals the radical nature of its heresy and its tendency toward the kind of common-sense liberalism that so deeply affected the nineteenth-century English-speaking world.

Mormonism was a [...] concept of classical [...] God as Eternal.

9. On Time and Eternity

IN ITS REJECTION of the classical concept of God as eternal, Mormonism is a most radical digression from traditional theism. This is perhaps its most important departure from familiar Christian orthodoxy, for it would be difficult to overestimate the importance to theology of the doctrine that God is a temporal being. It is not uncommon, of course, for the term "eternal" to be employed with the meaning of "everlasting," without end, or more especially without beginning or end. It has this connotation in typical Mormon discourse, where it carries as well the notion of ultimate worth. In technical metaphysics, however, eternity commonly means "timelessness," not in the sense of endless time but rather as indicating the nonreality of time as the succession of past, present, and future. In classical theism the idea of God's eternity is not that time is unreal for God but rather that, as eternal, God embraces the totality of time. Time is God's creation and therefore he is not subject to it. He transcends it.

Although Jewish theology, especially in late antiquity, became importantly involved with the concept of eternity, the typical descriptions of God occurring in the Old Testament are clearly temporalistic in character. More than anything else, God is described as a "living God," a divine person, a sovereign moral will who exists in time with a genuine past and a genuine future and projects his moral purposes in the human history that issues from the tension of the divine will with the freedom of man. God as highest reality is a living, dynamic, purposing being whose vitality is revealed in the processes of the natural world, in the moral decisions of men, and in the progressive movement of history.

The dominant trend in classical Greek metaphysics, in contrast, was impersonalistic rather than personalistic, intellectualistic rather than voluntaristic, and toward conceptions of ultimate reality as essentially static (being) rather than dynamic (becoming). In Platonism especially, the chief Hellenic influence on early Christian thought, the ultimately real, the intelligible world that is thought but not perceived, is motionless, timeless being — timeless because time can be defined only in terms of motion, and a world without motion, change, or process is therefore necessarily eternal. The story of classical Christian theology is in large part the story of a progressive attempt to describe the living, dynamic, temporal, personal God of the Hebrew religion by descriptions initially fashioned for the static, timeless, ultimate *being* of Greek metaphysics, a venture occasioned first by the conjunction of Greek and Hebraic culture in the Hellenistic and Roman worlds and one that inevitably built profound tensions into not only the Christian theology but as well into the whole structure of Christian culture.

In his effort to reconcile Greek metaphysics with biblical theology, Philo argued that "the great Cause of all things does not exist in time, nor at all in place, but he is superior to both time and place . . . . God is the creator of time also . . . so that there is nothing future to God, who has the very boundaries of time subject to him; . . . and in eternity nothing is past and nothing is future, but everything is present only." [27]

In the Eleventh Book of the *Confessions,* one of the most brilliant of all treatises on the nature of time, St. Augustine, in answer to the question: What was God doing before the creation of the world? described the eternity of God by asserting that God is the Lord of time, its creator, and that therefore there was no "before" the creation. For God there is neither past nor future, for "in the Eternal nothing passeth away, but . . . the whole is present." St. Thomas Aquinas defended the definition of the sixth-century Roman philosopher Boethius that "Eternity is the simultaneously-whole and perfect possession of interminable life" by arguing that in eternity there is no temporal succession. "The notion of eternity follows immutability, as the notion of time follows movement. . . . Hence, as God is supremely immutable, it supremely belongs to Him to be eternal." Aquinas argued that the temporal descriptions of God given in the Bible are not denials of his eternity but are employed "because His eternity includes all times. . . ."[28] "God . . . is entirely above the order of time. He is at the peak of eternity, surmounting everything all at once. Thence the stream of time can be seen in one simple glance."[29]

Orthodox Protestantism typically accepts a similar conception of God's eternity. In commenting on the nature of God's fore-knowledge, for instance, Calvin states, in the *Institutes of the Christian Religion*, "When we attribute foreknowledge to God, we mean that all things always were, and perpetually remain, under his eyes, so that to his knowledge there is nothing future or past, but all things are present. And they are present in such a way that he not only conceives them through ideas, as we have before us those things which our minds remember, but he truly looks upon them and discerns them as things placed before him."[30]

The idea of eternity is a difficult concept, and, although it is related in the classical theology to the common doctrine that God, as the creator of space, is not subject to space, being in a sense everywhere in general by virtue of being nowhere in particular, it has commonly been neglected by orthodox religious believers. They have usually failed to perceive that also by their theology, God, being "nowhen" in particular, is "everywhen" in general. There is no more fundamental problem in Christian theology than the relation of the eternal to the temporal, of God to the world and to the temporally contained human soul. It is, of course, a theological commonplace in Christianity that Christ is the intersection of time with eternity, for, according to the tradi-tional theology, in him the eternal God entered the domain of time to give meaning to human experience and human history. It is also a commonplace, derived especially from Christianity's ties with the temporally oriented Hebrew Bible, that God is in some way involved with man in the historical process, that his purposes are actualized and at least partially realized in time. But this serves simply to accentuate the theological problem of the relation of an eternal being, who is the creator of time and therefore not subject to it, to the time which he has created and which is the location of all his other creatures.

Now Mormonism has always assumed the naive concept of space and time as contexts for whatever is real. Accordingly, it denies eternity in the sense of timelessness, describing God as subject to both time and space. God is both somewhere and sometime, a view that has always widely prevailed in popular religion and that is central to the Mormon conception that God is a material being. The doctrine of God's temporality is the most radical facet of Mormon finitism and certainly the most important, for by its very nature temporality involves process, as the concept of time can have meaning only as a measure or context for events. God is placed therefore not above or without, but within the ongoing processes of the universe. The ultimate immutability of reality is thereby denied, and world history, human history, human effort, human achievement, and human freedom take on a new meaning, for the future is real and unique, not merely from the perspective of men, but as well from the perspective of God. On such a theory it should be impossible to bring men to subservience by the Spinozistic demand that they deny the verdict of their own experience by viewing themselves, their struggles, and their tragedies under the aspect of eternity, from the standpoint of an eternal God for whom there can be neither struggle nor tragedy. Rather, here God himself has the perspective of time, and whatever is in the world and whatever proceeds in the world is real for him genuinely and in its temporal process. The Mormon theologians seem generally to be unaware of the far-reaching implications of this distinctive facet of their theology, even though the Mormon religion is conducive to a highly sensitized temporal consciousness, as evidenced in the historical awareness that characterizes the Mormon mind and habit. Indeed, at times they even betray the high possibilities of their own theology by describing God as subject to eternal, immutable "principles" that are external to him, even though this relegates the divine personality to something less than the highest order of reality. They should find inspiration in Alfred North Whitehead's prophecy that "that religion will conquer which can render clear to popular understanding some eternal greatness incarnate in the passage of temporal fact."[31]

A notable attempt to resolve the eternity–time problem for Christian theology is Professor Paul Tillich's treatment of the issue in his *Systematic Theology*.[32] By its very nature, insists Tillich, eternity includes time. To call God eternal and yet affirm that he is a living God means that God includes temporality and is related to the modes of time.

It would be a serious error to suppose that the classical Christian doctrine was a denial of human history. On the contrary, it set the Hebrew time–history consciousness in firm opposition to the Greek and Roman conception of the cyclical nature of time that described history as turning indefinitely upon itself in an endless series of time cycles, a theory commonly accepted in the non-Semitic world and found in Thucydides, Plato, Aristotle, Lucretius, and the Stoics. This classical denial of history was finally overthrown by St. Augustine's *City of God*, which was a declaration of a temporal movement of human history from a beginning to an end, a process never to be repeated. The Hebrew conception of the world's beginning made it possible to conceive of an end, and with a beginning and an end there was a definite direction in the movement of history, a direction determined by the purposes or providence of God. But for Christianity, the historical process was nevertheless contained within the framework of eternity, and the numerous issues relating to the tensions of time and eternity were therefore inevitable.

10. On Nominalism and Materialism

MORMON THEOLOGY EXHIBITS no more obvious characteristic than its common-sense materialism and nominalism. In matters pertaining to religion the Mormon mind is typically given to the concrete and the particular and to physical imagery. It is direct, highly literalistic, and positivistic and tends to be sus-

picious of the abstract and recondite. It is typical of Mormon
theologians, therefore, to regard the traditional conceptions of
God that sustain a large element of Greek metaphysics as essentially meaningless. The central importance for the religion of the
first vision of Joseph Smith, together with a strong biblical literalism which favors especially the anthropomorphisms of the Hexa-
teuch, supports the conception of God as a material being existing
in space and time. This materialistic conception, of course, distinguishes Mormon theology from the traditional Christian theology which, influenced especially by Hellenistic Platonism and
by the Gnostic denials of the reality of matter, adopted the established Greek theory of the nature of reality as immaterial in its
higher forms.

The nominalistic and particularistic tendency of Mormon
thought, which so commonly insists that only the physically concrete is a genuinely real entity, is importantly exhibited in the
denial of the doctrine of the trinity as set forth by the Nicene
Creed, which is normative for both Catholicism and Protestantism. The orthodox trinitarian thesis of the Creed, which issued
from the early controversy over the nature of the divinity of
Christ, employs an Aristotelian conception of substance combined
with elements of Platonic and Aristotelian realism with their insistence on a genuine ontological status for universals. The Mormon doctrine is tritheistic, asserting the ontological independence
of the three divine persons, a doctrine traditionally declared
heretical. This anti-trinitarian position is consistent with the
nominalistic position that only particular objects and events have
reality. It is sometimes found associated with nominalism in the
history of Christian philosophy because a nominalistic metaphysics
necessarily denies the possibility of a universal substance over and
above the particularity of the three members of the Godhead.
The term "God" is not commonly used in Mormon discourse as
a synonym for "Godhead," for in Mormon terminology the latter
designates no subsistent entity but rather is a collective name
referring to the three divine persons taken as a unity, where the

ground of that unity is not a relation internal to their being that dissolves their ontological independence but is rather an external relationship involving total agreement in will and purpose.

The Mormon passion for concreteness is nowhere exhibited more clearly than in the vigorous polemics against classical theology that frequent its literature, especially as these are directed to the traditional formula set forth in the Anglican creed of 1571, "There is but one living and true God, everlasting, without body, parts, or passions. . . ."[33] Such a God, insist the Mormon theologians, claiming the support of both scripture and common sense, can be neither living nor everlasting, for whatever is without body or does not occupy space is nonexistent.

There is a sense in which many contemporary empiricists, especially the logical positivists, would agree in principle with this criticism, on the ground that operational definitions are not available for the term "God" as employed in the traditional formulae, that therefore the sentence "there is a God" is, in traditional theology, in principle unverifiable and consequently cognitively meaningless. However, the contention of some Mormon writers that the traditional thesis that God is an immaterial substance is a logical contradiction, is a simple error resulting from a failure to recognize that in technical metaphysical and theological discourse the terms "material" and "substance" are not equivalent in meaning. This same error was committed in the seventeenth century by Thomas Hobbes, the most celebrated materialist among modern philosophers. Hobbes considered the concept of immaterial substance to be self-contradictory and believed also, incidentally, that God must be a corporeal being since there is no other reality than matter in motion in space. The meaning of "substance" in philosophic discourse derives especially from Aristotelian metaphysics and logic and refers primarily to that which constitutes the essential being of an entity and which stands under and supports its observable attributes. By its very definition, such a substance may be conceived as immaterial. Now there may, in fact, be no immaterial substances such as the typical Christian theologians affirm, but the question of their existence or non-existence is one of fact, not of logic.

Since their views are drawn especially from the anthropomorphisms of the Bible and generally conform to common religious attitudes and concepts, it is not customary for Mormon writers to recognize the reasoning which historically supports such ideas as that God is without passions, a doctrine having a long and somewhat sophisticated history which involves especially Greek grammar, logic, and metaphysics. Its roots are in the Aristotelian dictum that God, being perfect, must be pure *act* and therefore free from every passive property. When the creeds say that God is without passions, the intended meaning is that he is always the subject and never the object, always *act* and never *acted upon*, a concept that obviously makes a stronger appeal within the context of abstract metaphysics than as a dictum referring to practical religion. In their opposition to such an element in the Christian creeds, the Mormons, who insist that if God is truly a person he must have passions, can take pleasure in Alfred North Whitehead's famous remark that Aristotle's "metaphysical train of thought . . . did not lead him very far towards the production of a God available for religious purposes."[34] Aristotle, of course, would have had contempt for the Christian idea that God is a person, and it is a grand irony that Christian theology has leaned so heavily upon his impersonalistic theory of the *Prime Mover*. But it is worthy of note that Whitehead pointed out that Aristotle in his treatment of the concept of God was himself without passions, and that he, who was the greatest metaphysician, was the "last European metaphysician of first-rate importance" to be "entirely dispassionate"[35] in dealing with this subject.

Or consider the creedal pronouncement that God is without "parts." Here again is a somewhat technical concept with sophisticated origins in Greek metaphysics that deserves to be understood by its critics. It can be seen for instance in Plato's *Phaedo*, where Socrates, awaiting execution, argues for the immortality of the soul (spirit) on the ground of its utter simplicity. The soul, he insisted, is a single, simple entity, not compounded of parts and therefore incapable of destruction, for destruction could occur only through disintegration and there can be no disintegration of whatever is simple rather than composite. The early Buddhist writings employ the same argument in reverse to establish that the soul is not immortal — that it is a compound of five elements and therefore disintegrates at death. Christian theology adopted the concept of the simplicity of God and the soul on the ground that only a being without parts could be imperishable.

It is interesting evidence of Mormonism's detachment from the mainstream of Christian thought that it should have committed itself to such a thoroughgoing materialism at the very time that materialism was increasingly identified with atheism. In general, late nineteenth-century materialism, usually associated with Newtonian physics and often also with Darwinian biology, was mechanistic in character. The opposition to religion generally associated with materialism, whether ancient or modern, has derived quite as much from the determinism implied by the theory of mechanical causation customary to materialistic metaphysics as from the concept that everything real, except space and time, is a mode of matter. The achievement near the close of the nineteenth century of a scientific synthesis which extended the mechanical theory — developed earlier in relation to terrestrial and celestial motions — to the entire domain of the physical sciences, and which brought under the dominion of mechanics even biology, psychology, and the social sciences, appeared to provide a solid foundation for a metaphysics that declared everything not definable ultimately in terms of physical and quantitative categories to be apparent only. The materialism that figures so prominently in Mormon thought is, of course, a radical departure from typical nineteenth-century materialism. The latter usually denies the reality of God and the soul, whereas Mormonism simply declares that God and the soul, or spirit, are material beings — composed of matter somewhat out of the ordinary, but material nevertheless.

Moreover, the Mormon theologians have attempted to avoid any mechanistic implications of their materialism that would deny either human freedom of will in the libertarian sense or the creative freedom of God. The highly speculative materialism of Orson Pratt, which has in a general way profoundly influenced Mormon thought though it was never accepted as an official Church position, draws heavily on Newtonian concepts but is essentially panpsychistic in character. In the latter respect it exhibits interesting similarities to ancient Milesian hylozoism and, as already indicated, to the Leibnizian theory of monads. For Pratt, reality is material and atomistic, each individual atom possessing powers of intelligent action and self-direction. In contrast to Leibniz' monads, however, Pratt's atoms constitute an inter-communicating community, and in contrast to both the pre-established harmony of Leibniz and ordinary mechanical determinism, Pratt's atoms behave freely in a manner proposed but not necessitated by the divine will. Their behavior, when considered collectively, is described as natural law. (Cf., "Absurdities of Immaterialism" and "Great First Cause," *passim.*)

Such a theory has a flavor somewhat suggestive of the concept of indeterminacy that some have derived from Heisenberg's principle of uncertainty. But Pratt's ideas, published around 1850, are severely conditioned by the now outmoded Newtonian concepts of absolute space and time and by the early pre-Rutherford concept of atoms. Moreover, his logic, which assumed the possibility of establishing factual premises axiomatically, is now known to be fundamentally in error. (Cf. esp., "Great First Cause," pp. 1–2.) The Mormon pioneers for whom Pratt wrote, while delighting in intellectual adventure, were not especially partial to the doctrine that sticks and stones are composed of little living souls.

A second serious but also abortive attempt to establish a metaphysics for Mormonism was that of William H. Chamberlin, who, writing in the first decades of the present century, had scientific preoccupations with psychology and biology and the problems of evolution and theology rather than with physics and the problems of mechanism and determinism. Chamberlin, however, who was influenced especially by Josiah Royce and George Holmes Howison, was essentially a personalistic idealist whose philosophy was associated historically with the grand attack upon materialism and naturalism which characterized British and American metaphysical idealism at the turn of the century. Though his conception of God, being finitistic and personalistic, fully conformed to the outlines of Mormon orthodoxy, as did his liberal concept of man, the idealistic facets of Chamberlin's metaphysics stood out in sharp contrast to the materialism to which the Mormon mind had become accustomed and which it even now regards as firmly grounded in revelation, science, and common sense. (Cf. Ralph V. Chamberlin, *The Life and Philosophy of W. H. Chamberlin.*)

Although naturalistic metaphysics is perhaps more firmly established now than ever before, much that characterized the old nineteenth-century materialism, as exhibited for instance in the work of Ludwig Buchner and Ernst Haeckel, has been discredited by twentieth-century relativity physics and quantum mechanics. Considering the countless problems posed for theology by the crudities of the now scientifically outmoded conception of matter as space-filling stuff, and considering also the large measure of philosophical activity that has been generated by the new theories of matter, space, and time — to say nothing of the revolutionary developments in biophysics — it is somewhat surprising that no serious attempt has been made to ground Mormon metaphysics and theology in a more scientifically acceptable and philosophically justifiable type of materialism. Granted that Mormon orthodoxy demands a materialistic metaphysics, there is certainly nothing about it that necessitates allegiance to a scientifically obsolete approach to the nature of matter and the structure of the natural universe.

11. On Natural Theology

THE PRIMARY TASK OF THEOLOGY is to reconcile the revelation to the culture, to make what is taken on faith as the word of God meaningful in the light of accepted science and philosophy. Mormonism has little traffic with the major philosophical trends of our time, and generally views the philosophical systems with considerable suspicion. Nevertheless, there have been some efforts in the past to construct a natural or rational theology for Mormonism, although in view of the religion's primary emphasis on revelation those efforts were perhaps at times misdirected except as rationalizations of the doctrine. There is among the Mormons a pronounced intellectualism in matters pertaining to religion and a strong commitment to the capacities of human reason. It is assumed that the world is intelligible and though there are limitations to human knowledge in relation to the objects of religion, those limitations do not justify the acceptance of paradox or an official doctrine of mysteries. In principle everything is knowable and the ways of God are reasonable.

The history of Catholic philosophy is in part the story of the effort to determine the proper relation of knowledge to faith, to determine the ground of knowledge, its basis in reason and experience, its capacities and limitations, and its relations to revealed truth. It is commonly held in Catholicism, for instance, that it is possible by the unaided reason to prove the existence of God. According to St. Thomas Aquinas this can be done especially by the traditional Greek cosmological and teleological arguments, arguments based on the causal order of the world and on the evidences in nature of purposive adaptation to ends. But the nature of God, as for instance that he is one in substance and three in persons, cannot be fully understood by human reason and must be accepted on faith.

In modern Protestantism the knowledge–faith issue takes a variety of forms and it is not possible, therefore, to generalize on it.

A most important development, however, was the large impact of Immanuel Kant on Protestant thought. Kant's analysis of the nature of knowledge led him to the conclusion that a rational proof of the existence of God is an impossibility and that God must be taken, therefore, as an object of faith rather than knowledge.

In Mormonism there is no official position on these matters, but it is commonly held by the Mormon theologians that the cosmological and teleological arguments have value. Their value, however, is not that they are firm and conclusive proofs of God's existence but rather are rational supports of the claims of revelation. Both the existence and nature of God are known by revelation only. In this way the primacy of revelation is protected.

PART THREE

THE CONCEPT OF MAN

12. On The Self as a Necessary Existent

THE MORMON CONCEPT OF MAN is distinguished from the classical Christian doctrine primarily in its denial that man is essentially and totally a creature of God. This follows from the fundamental thesis of Mormon metaphysics that all primary being is original and uncreated. In contrast to the view of traditional Christianity, both Catholic and Protestant, Mormonism describes all reality in its constituent elements as ultimately uncreated and imperishable. The most important facet of this denial of origins, with radical meanings for the Mormon religion as well as for the theology, is the doctrine that the human self in its essential being is given and uncreated. Moreover, the self is not identified with a world soul or substance or universal psyche, as in some forms of theosophy and pantheism. Nor is it a derivative or emanation from an absolute which is thereby the ground of its being, as in Neoplatonism. Nor is it a facet, part, mode, or aspect of a single divine reality with which it enjoys an ontological identity, as in Spinoza and much oriental thought. On the contrary, the Mormon view of the nature of the self or of the individual personality is grounded in a pluralistic metaphysics which guarantees that full individuality is a necessary property of every person. Whatever is essential to at least the elementary being of the individual person in his full particularity, therefore, existing in the most ultimate and mysterious sense, is uncreated, underived, and unbegun. Here Mormonism is basically at variance not only with traditional Christian theology, which in both its Catholic and Protestant forms affirms the special *ex nihilo* creation of the soul, but with occidental philosophy generally, both sacred and secular.

With reference to the question of the creation of man, *The Doctrine and Covenants* asserts that "Man was also in the beginning with God. Intelligence, or the light of truth, was not created or made, neither indeed can be."[1] In support of the doctrine that this uncreated intelligence is the individual ego and not simply some kind of world soul, Mormon theology has drawn especially on the later teachings of the Mormon prophet Joseph Smith. Shortly before his death in 1844, in a discourse that has received official Church authentication and has had a profound influence on Mormon thought, the Prophet made a number of statements pertinent to the idea that in its essential being the human self is not created and contingent.

> We say that God Himself is a self-existing being. . . . Who told you that man did not exist in like manner upon the same principles? Man does exist upon the same principles. . . . The mind or the intelligence which man possesses is co-equal with God himself. . . . The intelligence of spirits had no beginning, neither will it have an end. . . . The first principles of man are self-existent with God.[2]

Although the idea that the self is uncreated and without temporal beginning is uncommon in Western thought, independently of its late introduction through the importation of oriental religion and philosophy, it is not entirely unknown. Origen, in the third century, argued for the preexistence of all rational souls, a position that exhibited the influence of Platonism upon him and may have been received by him from his teacher Clement of Alexandria. But for Origen, as for most Christian theologians, the world had a beginning in time and in his view the souls were created by God at the creation of the world at the beginning of time. "They [rational creatures] existed undoubtedly from the very beginning in those [ages] which are not seen, and are eternal."[3] The teaching of Origen was eventually declared heretical, and although the doctrine of preexistence appeared from time to time among the patristics and found a place even in the Talmud, it was effectively suppressed in the Catholic Church at least from the sixth century.

There are, however, interesting instances in recent metaphysics of the idea that the self is uncreated and unbegun which have some similarity to the Mormon view. The distinguished Scottish philosopher J. M. E. McTaggart (1866–1925), while denying the existence of God, held that the individual personality in its ultimate being is a given element in reality, uncreated and indestructible. McTaggart's argument is related to his treatment of the problem of time and consists basically of insisting that the nature of man is such that it necessarily involves a life both before and after the present life. (Cf. John McTaggart Ellis McTaggart, *Human Immortality and Pre-Existence*.)

A theory in some ways closer to the Mormon doctrine, because of its affirmation of theism, was advanced and aggressively defended by Howison, one of the foremost American philosophers of his time. Both McTaggart and Howison were intensely pluralistic and personalistic in their metaphysics, insisting that individual personalities are the primary uncreated ingredients of the universe. For Howison, as for Mormon theology, God and the community of selves simply exist. There is no more occasion to explain their existence than there is to account for the existence of God in the traditional theism. Howison does not hold a commonplace theory of the preexistence of souls, however, for his Kantian concept of time subordinates time to personality, which is taken as eternal, or timeless. "A soul or mind or person, purely as such, is itself the fountain of its percipient experience, and so possesses what has been happily named 'life in itself.' "[4]

Howison speaks of "self-active causes" and "the imperishable self-resource of the individual spirit." He sets his pluralistic system against every form of metaphysical absolutism. "The many Primary Realities, when we discover them in their undermost foundations, are all rational intelligences, and . . . they therefore spontaneously constitute, not indeed any Unit, in which their freedom would be swamped and crushed, but a rational Union, or Harmony, which is therefore as indestructible as they are."[5]

If the question is asked: What is the nature of the uncreated self in Mormon metaphysics? it is entirely compatible with the whole spirit of the philosophy and theology, and it conforms to the almost obsessive Mormon concern for free moral agency, to reply that the individual self is identified especially with freedom of will, the person in the fullest sense being largely characterized by, if not identical with, that freedom and its consequences. Here is the ontological ground of the Mormon humanism that opposes not only the classical doctrine of original sin and all which that concept implies for both theology and the moral and spiritual life, but contradicts as well the negative description of the human predicament that lies at the center of both secular existentialism and all forms of the new existentialist orthodoxy.

The Protestant Christian existentialist analysis of the human predicament in terms of the creatureliness of man and the anxiety arising from his contingency has received what may be its definitive statement in the theology of the German-American theologian Paul Tillich. "The doctrine of man's creatureliness," says Tillich, "is another point in the doctrine of man where nonbeing has a dialectical character. Being created out of nothing means having to return to nothing. The stigma of having originated out of nothing is impressed on every creature."[6] He goes on to say:

> The anxiety in which causality is experienced is that of not being in, of, and by one's self, of not having the "aseity" which theology traditionally attributes to God. Man is a creature. His being is contingent; by itself it has no necessity, and therefore man realizes that he is the prey of nonbeing. The same contingency which has thrown man into existence may push him out of it. . . . The anxiety in which

he is aware of this situation is anxiety about the lack of necessity of his being.[7]

The threat of non-being that, except for the grace of God, dominates created man is similarly expressed in the work of Karl Barth, the most influential of the contemporary neoorthodox theologians. "The creature is threatened by the possibility of nothingness and of destruction, which is excluded by God — and only by God. If a creature exists, it is only maintained in its mode of existence if God so wills. If He did not so will, nothingness would inevitably break in from all sides. The creature itself could not rescue and preserve itself."[8]

The neoorthodox philosopher Emil Brunner, in his major work, *Man in Revolt*, has summarized this issue in terms of the radical ontological distinction between man and God.

> There is no greater sense of distance than that which lies in the words Creator-Creation. Now this is the first and the fundamental thing which can be said about man: He is a creature, and as such he is separated by an abyss from the Divine manner of being. The greatest dissimilarity between two things which we can express at all — more dissimilar than light and darkness, death and life, good and evil — is that between the Creator and that which is created.[9]

Catholic theology, even where it reflects the impact of modern existentialism, is somewhat more moderate in its description of the relation of creature to creator, the moderation following especially from its emphasis on the essential nature of existent being and its common rejection of the existentialist dictum that existence is prior to essence. Nevertheless, the ultimately full contingency of man is affirmed by all Catholic theologians, and God is described as the only absolutely necessary being. Aquinas employed as his third argument for God the requirement for an absolute necessity to account for the existence of contingent being. "Therefore we cannot but admit the existence of some being having of itself its own necessity, and not receiving it from another, but rather causing in others their necessity. This all men speak of as God."[10]

Modern liberal Protestantism has generally played down the ontological distance between man and God, not so much by explicit theological pronouncements as by tempering both the practical and theoretical stress on the creatureliness of man and by a not uncommon association with idealistic metaphysics, which is not especially congenial to the traditional doctrine of creation. There has also been an association with forms of mysticism that are even less congenial, and at times with theories of emergent evolution which demand a radical reconsideration of the entire concept of origins.

At the heart of its ontological doctrine, Mormonism is in fundamental opposition to existentialism and neoorthodoxy, for it denies the very predicament of man that they in all their forms affirm: the fact of man's utter contingency. In Mormon doctrine, the individual has necessary being. He exists *necessarily.* That is, he could not *not* exist. Whatever the activity of God in determining or affecting the condition of man, God is not ultimately a creator and every man has the ground of his own being within himself. Whatever the predicament of man, it does not arise from an essential insecurity in his being. However finite and involved with finitude, the existence of man is not precarious or in doubt, because his existence is given as a central and irreducible fact of reality. Insofar, then, as the consciousness of natural guilt or of the meaninglessness of existence or the anguish of death and extinction are rooted in the ontological danger of creaturely finitude, these find no metaphysical support in Mormon theology. On the contrary, it is clear that the characteristic life affirmations of the Mormon religion, together with the typical preoccupation with actual rather than original sin and guilt, are compatible with and, in the subtle ways that relate theory to practice, draw support from the fundamental concept of the uncreated self.

It is this concept of man as uncreated and underived, a necessary being standing ontologically with God and the world, that

constitutes the radical heresy of Mormonism against the traditional Christian faith. It is not only a fundamental departure
from the established doctrine of man, for it entails the denial of
the absoluteness of God and justifies also the denial of the doctrine
of salvation by the divine grace only. When judged by Augustinian Christianity, Mormonism, at least in its metaphysics, is clearly
guilty of the traditional Christian sin of pride, the first of the
deadly sins, the denial of creatureliness and all that this entails.
The fundamentalist theology has defined and established this sin
by its consistent denigration of human nature. Augustine, Luther,
Calvin, and, in a sense, even Aquinas, follow Paul in rooting even
sensual sin in the pride of an inordinate self-esteem and ambition
and a failure to sense the limitations of human freedom. "There
is a pride of power," says Reinhold Niebuhr, in *The Nature and
Destiny of Man*, "in which the human ego assumes its self-suffi-
ciency and self-mastery and imagines itself secure against all
vicissitudes. It does not recognize the contingent and dependent
character of its life and believes itself to be the author of its own
existence, the judge of its own values and the master of its own
destiny."[11]

Niebuhr's statement, a product on the one hand of a profound
historical and psychological analysis of human motivation and on
the other of the disillusionment and disenchantment attending the
dramatic human failures of the twentieth century, is at least a
partially acceptable polemic against the superficial facets of the
liberal estimate of man. But it does not justly describe liberalism,
either religious or secular. For the liberal conception of man,
whatever its excesses in overstating the possibilities of social
progress and its deficiencies in understanding the fact of personal
as well as social guilt, did not encourage the individual to suppose
himself self-sufficient, secure against all vicissitudes, or free from
all contingency. Certainly it defined the good life in terms of
positive personal satisfactions rather than denials, and encouraged a strong confidence in the possibilities of human virtue and
the capacities of human reason. But whether one considers liber-

alism in Judaism, Protestantism, Catholicism, or even contemporary naturalistic humanism, he will find that those who seriously presume the role of God are eccentrics. A sense of dependence and insufficiency and a recognition of contingent danger are not exclusive to the orthodox fundamentalist.

The Mormon conception of the nature and predicament of man is rooted in more than the pluralistic metaphysics that logically supports Mormon liberalism. It is in part the product of the nineteenth-century spirit of enlightenment and the commitment to the expansive possibilities of human freedom that have generally characterized American thought and attitude. But it is affected also by the centuries-old Christian tradition that denies liberalism and it is set in fundamentalist theological forms that effectively contain it. Although Mormon doctrine holds that the person ultimately is uncreated and indestructible, it nevertheless holds as well that the soul is subject to salvation, and in a very unorthodox sense to damnation, and that, although man's ultimate destiny is determined not by divine decree but by human merit, salvation is possible only through Jesus Christ and by the grace of God. Though the faithful Mormon faces life and death with a large measure of confidence in himself and his fellow men, and this unquestionably is at times a confidence that is proud and unjustifiably optimistic, he has, nevertheless, a profound sense of dependence upon God for his present estate and for whatever salvation he may achieve.

The Mormon religion is oriented generally to the affirmative spirit of the Hebrew prophets and Jesus, rather than to the negations of Paul and the theologians. It has celebrated the relative independence and powers of the human spirit, and at times it has greatly exaggerated those powers by a legalistic approach to the relation of man to God. Nevertheless, neither this nor the doctrine of the uncreated self has resulted in a concept of the divine–human relationship that is in principle foreign to familiar liberal theism. There is here not a sense of the total otherness of God and therefore there is not that consciousness of abject creatureliness that generates the guilt that attaches to existence itself. There is rather a sense of familial community with God and Christ that encourages a belief in the ultimate worth of the individual and in the surpassing importance of his free involvement in the divine purpose. Here, as at many other points, Mormonism has much in common with typical liberal Protestantism. The Mormon doctrine insists emphatically on the continuity of the human with the divine and lays great stress on the ultimate possibilities of the development of the divine potential in human nature in the course of an endless progress in which man, God, and the total cosmos are involved. This faith, which appears at times in a quite extravagant form, quite certainly was encouraged by the historical optimism that dominated the American mind in the nineteenth century.

13. On Original Sin

THE CENTRAL DOGMA of traditional Christian orthodoxy is the doctrine of original sin. From it follows the doctrine of salvation by the grace of God only. As a consequence of the sin of the first man, human nature in its very being is sinful, and every man from the moment of his creation, therefore, is by nature sinful and is set against God, impotent to merit salvation and worthy only of an eternal damnation and punishment. The general structure of Christian theology and also most Christian ecclesiastical forms are derived from or intimately related to this negative assessment of man and his predicament.

The classical form of the doctrines of original sin and salvation by grace, which are grounded in part in the fifth chapter of *The Epistle to the Romans*, was set forth in the fifth century by St. Augustine, especially in the essays *On Nature and Grace* and *On the Grace of Christ and On Original Sin*, which were written in opposition to Pelagianism. The British monk Pelagius aroused much intellectual excitement in Rome and North Africa in the first two decades of the fifth century by denying both original sin and the doctrine of salvation by grace and arguing persuasively for the doctrine of salvation by merit.

> Everything good and everything evil, in respect of which we are either worthy of praise or of blame, is *done by us*, not *born with us*. We are not born in our full development, but with a capacity for good and evil; we are begotten as well without virtue as without vice, and before the activity of our own personal will there is nothing in man but what God has stored in him.[12]

A set of theses prepared against Celestius, a disciple of Pelagius, by Paulinus of Milan in A.D. 411–12 summarizes the chief heresies of the Pelagian beliefs:

1. Adam was created mortal, and he would have died, whether he sinned or not.
2. Adam's sin injured himself alone, not the human race.
3. The Law, as well as the Gospel, leads to the Kingdom.
4. There were men without sin before Christ's coming.
5. New-born infants are in the same condition as Adam before the Fall.
6. It is not through the death or the fall of Adam that the whole human race dies, nor through the resurrection of Christ that the whole human race rises again.

> Certain other points were raised against him, put forward on the mention of my name . . . ;
>
> That a man can be without sin, if he choose.
>
> That infants, even if unbaptized, have eternal life.
>
> That rich men who have been baptized are not credited with any good that they may seem to have done, unless they give up all they have; not otherwise can they enter the Kingdom of God.[13]

Pelagius avoided condemnation by the Synod of Jerusalem in A.D. 415, but his teachings were condemned by the Council of Carthage in A.D. 416, and in A.D. 417 he and his disciple Celestius were excommunicated by Pope Innocent I. Again in A.D. 418 a council at Carthage condemned his teachings and issued a statement of nine canons relating to the subject. The Pelagian heresy exhibited occasional strength until its disappearance late in the sixth century after numerous investigations and condemnations.

St. Augustine's attacks upon Pelagius and his disciples were decisive for the Church in the fifth century and have in varying degrees carried great authority ever since, in Protestantism as well as Catholicism. Augustine refused to grant the basic assumption of Pelagianism, that the doctrines of original sin and grace vitiate the fact of moral responsibility, and insisted that the very movement of the soul toward God comes only as a gift of God and not as an act of free will. He was quite prepared to accept the dogma of predestination that this implied, though in general it was not popular in the Church, for here he relied heavily upon his own experience of total helplessness and dependence upon God rather than upon any philosophical consideration of the nature of the moral life such as had determined the thought of Pelagius.

For Augustine, whose theological ideas have been the most influential in Christendom, religion is essentially an inward disposition, and theology is rooted more in psychological than in philosophical, social, or historical considerations. The soul stands convicted of its guilt in the presence of God, yet experiences the grace of God. This is the substance of religion, for which Augustine claims not only the authenticating force of his own experience of conversion, but scriptural authority of the Apostle in Romans 3:23-24: "For all have sinned, and come short of the glory of God; Being justified freely by his grace through the redemption that is in Christ Jesus."

Augustine's central theological ideas were never finalized in a completed, closed, and internally consistent system. They took shape often in the heat of controversy and they reflect the extremes of the powerful emotions of one who had the intellectual strength to impose his own inner convictions upon the whole subsequent history of Christian civilization. In summary, his doctrine of man and salvation is the general format of Christian fundamentalism: that as a consequence of Adam's sin, freely committed, the entire human race is one mass of sin (*massa peccati*), deserving only damnation and morally and spiritually impotent to merit salvation. But with an unmerited mercy, God in his goodness and in his inscrutable wisdom has elected some to salvation, while all others are consigned justly to an everlasting perdition. Even the faith in Christ through whom the divine grace is communicated is available only to those who from the beginning are predestined by God for salvation. Those whom God has elected to damnation cannot in any way by an act of moral will or faith initiate the gift of grace, but those whom he has created for salvation are without power to thwart that grace, for it is irresistible and the saints can do nothing but persevere.

> Since they will not in fact persevere unless they both *can* and *will* . . . their will is so kindled by the Holy Spirit that they *can*, just because they *will*, and they *will* just because *God works in them so to will.*[14]

Although Catholicism in time rejected the extremes of the Augustinian doctrine, as for instance belief in predestination to damnation, the impact of Augustine was permanent. The Augustinian concept of man and his predicament had a genuine rebirth in the theology of the major Protestant reformers of the sixteenth century and at times enjoyed some acceptance even within the camp of Catholicism, as with the heretical Jansenist movement of the seventeenth century. In the *Institutes of the Christian Religion*, first published in 1536, Calvin holds that original sin "seems to be"

> A hereditary depravity and corruption of our nature, diffused into all parts of the soul, which first makes us liable to God's wrath. . . . First, we are so vitiated and perverted in every part of our nature that by this great corruption we stand justly condemned and convicted before God, to whom nothing is acceptable but righteousness, innocence, and purity. . . . For our nature is not only destitute and empty of good, but so fertile and fruitful of every evil

that it cannot be idle. Those who have said that original sin is 'concupiscence' [esp. Augustine] have used an appropriate word, if only it be added . . . that whatever is in man, from the understanding to the will, from the soul even to the flesh, has been defiled and crammed with his concupiscence. Or, to put it more briefly, the whole man is of himself nothing but concupiscence.[15]

The *Augsburg Confession*, the most important symbol of evangelical Protestantism, written in 1530 by Melanchthon on a foundation of Luther's doctrines and approved by Luther, agrees in principle with the later statement of Calvin.

Also they teach that, after Adam's fall, all men begotten after the common course of nature are born with sin; that is, without the fear of God, without trust in him, and with fleshly appetite; and that this disease, or original fault, is truly sin, condemning and bringing eternal death now also upon all that are not born again by baptism and the Holy Spirit.

They condemn the Pelagians, and others, who deny this original fault to be sin indeed; and who, so as to lessen the glory of the merits and benefits of Christ, argue that a man may, by the strength of his own reason, be justified before God.[16]

The Augustinian conception of original sin appears also in the basic Anglican creed, *The Thirty-Nine Articles of Religion of the Church of England*, published in 1571. The American revision of 1801 for the Protestant Episcopal Church in the United States of America reads as follows:

Original sin standeth not in the following of Adam (as the Pelagians do vainly talk) ; but it is the fault and corruption of the Nature of every man, that naturally is engendered of the offspring of Adam; whereby man is very far gone from original righteousness, and is of his own nature inclined to evil, so that the flesh lusteth always contrary to the spirit; and therefore in every person born into this world, it deserveth God's wrath and damnation. . . .[17]

The same Augustinian doctrine dominates the most important Puritan creed, *The Westminster Confession of Faith* of 1647, the chief doctrinal standard for Scottish and American Presbyterianism.

> By this sin they [our first parents] fell from their original righteousness and communion with God, and so became dead in sin, and wholly defiled in all the faculties and parts of soul and body. They being the root of all mankind, the guilt of this sin was imputed, and the same death in sin and corrupted nature conveyed to all their posterity descending from them by ordinary generation.[18]

Contemporary Protestant neoorthodox thought rejects the historicity of the biblical account of the fall of man but nevertheless regards that account as symbolic of the most profound truth on the human predicament. It has generally, therefore, placed the doctrine of original sin at the center of its polemic against liberalism. Original sin is described especially in terms of human estrangement and rebellion against God rather than as the Augustinian concupiscence with its sensual implications. Paul Tillich, for instance, describes original or hereditary sin as "neither original nor hereditary; it is the universal destiny of estrangement which concerns every man."[19] It is man's estrangement from his essential nature and from the ground of his being, arising from his existential finitude, that produces anxiety and despair. (Cf. esp., Paul Tillich, *The Courage To Be*.)

Emil Brunner opposes the traditional Augustinian concept of original sin as non-biblical, insisting that the concern for concupiscence is essentially Hellenistic in origin. The biblical view, he insists, "regards Sin, essentially, as defiance and arrogance."[20]

Catholicism historically rejected the extreme Augustinian doctrine of original sin in favor of a compromise with Pelagianism that yielded a more moderate conception of the human predicament. In conformity with the Augustinian tendency to define evil negatively rather than positively, original sin is described as the loss of something that had been added to the human nature.

It is the culpable deprivation of the supernatural gift of sanctifying grace, without which man cannot transcend the limitations
of his finite nature. St. Thomas Aquinas and some others have
added the deprivation of integrity, which in positive terms is the
existence of concupiscence. But the Catholic Church rejects
vehemently the Protestant doctrine that original sin is an essential
corruption of the human soul. It belongs to all men by virtue of
their descendance from Adam and is in the essence of the soul
and not simply the flesh. But because it is essentially the loss of
a supernatural gift added to human nature, it is not in itself a
total depravity of that nature. As it has sometimes been stated
by Catholic writers, human nature is wounded but not corrupted
by the sin of Adam. Following Aristotle, Catholic philosophy
defines human nature primarily in terms of rationality, and
Aquinas declares, for instance, that ". . . sin cannot entirely take
away from man the fact that he is a rational being, for then he
would no longer be capable of sin. Therefore it is not possible for
this good of nature to be entirely destroyed."[21]

The dogma of original sin was set forth for Catholic believers
by the Council of Trent in its fifth session in 1546, in part as
follows:

> If any one does not confess that the first man, Adam,
> when he had transgressed the commandment of God in
> Paradise, immediately lost the holiness and justice wherein
> he had been constituted; and that he incurred, through the
> offense of that prevarication, the wrath and indignation of
> God, and consequently death, with which God had pre-
> viously threatened him, and, together with death, captivity
> under his power who thenceforth *had the empire of death,*
> *that is to say, the devil,* and that the entire Adam, through
> that offense of prevarication, was changed, in body and
> soul, for the worse; let him be anathema.
>
> If any one asserts, that the prevarication of Adam
> injured himself alone, and not his posterity; and that the
> holiness and justice, received of God, which he lost, he lost
> for himself alone, and not for us also; or that he, being
> defiled by the sin of disobedience, has only transfused death

and pains of the body into the whole human race, but not sin also, which is death of the soul; let him be anathema.[22]

Catholic theologians commonly hold that a complaint of injustice cannot properly be made on the ground that the individual is deprived of grace for no actual sin of his own, because the soul has no rights to that grace since it was bestowed entirely as a free supernatural gift and does not belong to human nature as such.

Arising amid the decline of American Calvinism and within the world that produced both secular and religious liberalism, Mormonism from its origins has been grounded in an affirmative doctrine of man and his predicament that denies original sin while accepting literally the biblical account of Adam. This has necessitated a paradoxical interpretation of the fall as conforming to the divine will, an interpretation that has centered on the idea that the fall was essential to the moral development of the human soul. This is a radical departure from the foundations of classical theology, a departure that partially identifies Mormonism with the tradition of liberal religion and excludes it from the category of typical fundamentalism despite its Christology and biblical literalism.

The term "original sin" is occasionally encountered in Mormon literature, especially of the earlier period, but in Mormon terminology it usually refers simply to the first sin, the sin of Adam, with no meaning whatsoever for the sinfulness by nature of the generality of men. This is evident, for example, in the following from the discourses of Brigham Young: ". . . [The] Savior . . . came in the meridian of time to redeem the earth and the children of men from the original sin that was committed by our first parents."[23] No other meaning is possible to a theology that emphatically denies the possibility of any involvement of mankind in the sin of Adam.

Of the thirteen Articles of Faith, which were written informally by Joseph Smith and function for the non-creedal Mormons as a kind of unofficial but accepted creed, the second is: "We believe that men will be punished for their own sins, and not for Adam's transgression." Most Mormon writers seem to have been unaware that in the classical theology men are not typically held responsible for Adam's sin, but rather for their own original sinfulness which they possess by virtue of the "solidarity" of mankind in Adam as the progenitor of the race. The Lutheran *Formula of Concord*, written in 1576, asserts: "We therefore reject and condemn that dogma by which it is asserted that Original Sin is merely the liability and debt of another's transgression, transmitted to us apart from any corruption of our nature."[24] In Catholic teaching the individual will is not responsible for the state of sinfulness, because it was not an "actual" sin. Adam's will, nevertheless, was in a sense a "family" will. This concept of solidarity in Adam, though uncommon in Mormon thought, is not totally absent. Consider, for instance, the comment of Joseph F. Smith, the sixth president of the Mormon Church, on the fact of mortality: " 'In the day that thou eatest thou shalt surely die.' This was the edict of the Almighty, and it pertains to Adam — that is, all the human race; for Adam is many, and it means you and me and every soul that lives and that bears the image of the Father."[25]

The typical Mormon view, nevertheless, is that expressed by the Mormon apostle James E. Talmage. "If the expression 'original sin' has any definite signification it must be taken to mean the transgression of our parents in Eden. We were not participators in that offense. We are not inheritors of original sin, though we be subjects of the consequences."[26] Talmage also comments that "Belief in original sin, with its dread incubus as a burden from which none can escape, has for ages cast its depressing shadow over the human heart and mind."[27]

It is essential to the traditional meaning of original sin, both Catholic and Protestant, that the condition of sinfulness attaches as a quality or property to every person simply by virtue of his humanness. Original sin is a state of his being — in Protestant orthodoxy, a natural corruption and depravity; in Catholicism, a deprivation of the supernatural; but in each a quality that inheres in every man from birth — a sin for which every man is born responsible and for which he merits punishment. For Mormonism this has no meaning. The only sin is the actual sin that a man commits, not in some mystical sense as a participant in Adam's sin, but in his own freedom by his own determination. Adam's sin can and does have consequences for man, e.g., mortality and spiritual death, but a state of culpable sinfulness, conceived either negatively or positively, cannot be among those consequences.

It should be noted here that it is typical of Protestant theology to exempt Christ from original sin by virtue of his divinity. Catholicism holds in addition that the Mother of Christ was, by a divine miracle, free from original sin. This latter is the doctrine of the Immaculate Conception, a doctrine sometimes confused with the doctrine of the Virgin Birth of Christ. The Mormon theology accepts the doctrine of the Virgin Birth but has no place, of course, for the concept of the Immaculate Conception. Belief in the freedom of the Virgin from original sin was a matter of dispute for many centuries in the Catholic Church until a decree of Pius IX in 1854 promulgated the definition of the Immaculate Conception. Taken from the Papal Bull *Ineffabilis Deus,* the definition reads in part: ". . . that the doctrine which holds the Blessed Virgin Mary to have been, from the first instant of her conception, by a singular grace and privilege of Almighty God, in view of the merits of Christ Jesus the Saviour of mankind, preserved free from all stain of original sin, was revealed by God, and is, therefore, to be firmly and constantly believed by all the faithful."

To fail to recognize that at its foundations Mormon theology is essentially a rebellion against especially the orthodox Protestant dogma of original sin, and the negativism implied by it for the interpretation of the whole nature and life of man, would be a failure to discern not only the distinctive character of Mormon doctrine but also of the Mormon religion itself. As indicated earlier, Mormon theology is set in the classical Christian framework defined by the fall of man in Adam and the atonement through Jesus Christ. But the Mormon character developed against a background of American dissent and rationalism. And above all, it had its beginnings in an atmosphere of optimism that rejected the life-denying qualities of traditional Puritanism. The biblical literalism that fed it was characterized less by the negative theology of Paul than by the life affirmations of Jesus and the prophets. Inevitably it was a central task of the Mormon theologians to accommodate their liberal concept of man to the limitations imposed by the doctrines of the fall and the atonement that had for fifteen hundred years dominated Christian orthodoxy with a somewhat negative appraisal of man and his predicament. The history of Mormon theology, therefore, has been at many points a recasting of Pelagianism, Socinianism, or Arminianism in a nineteenth-twentieth-century role, but where reason and theological subtleties have counted for less than common-sense insights, practical necessities, and dogmatic certainties.

Now Mormon literature is not entirely free of the concept of original sin and the particular Christological concepts that it has traditionally implied. This is especially true of the *Book of Mormon*, which abounds with references to the fall and the atonement. It is difficult, for example, to attach any other meaning to Mosiah 3:19, "For the natural man is an enemy to God, and has been from the fall of Adam, and will be, forever and ever, unless he yields to the enticings of the Holy Spirit, and putteth off the natural man and becometh a saint through the atonement of Christ the Lord. . . ." Moreover, there is currently a kind of Jansenist movement in Mormon academic circles that appears to be dedicated to the celebration of whatever Augustinian elements may be discernible in the scriptures, a movement that, not unexpectedly, is placing some emphasis on the *Epistle to the Romans*. Nevertheless, such negativism in the assessment of man, whether scriptural or otherwise, is a betrayal of the spirit and

dominant character not only of the Mormon theology but also of
the Mormon religion, which draws heavily on doctrinal foundations in supporting its practical affirmation of man and its positive moral ideal.

Since the origins of Mormon theology are enmeshed in the
movement of American Protestant dissent in the early nineteenth
century, numerous tendencies of that period are discernible in
the early Mormon literature. But from at least the time of Joseph
Smith's Nauvoo sermons, where the outlines of a dogmatic metaphysics are clearly discernible, a liberal doctrine of man has been
increasingly written into the foundations of the theology, a doctrine conformable to the life-affirming spirit that has always
characterized the Mormon people and informed the Mormon
community. As early as 1837, Parley P. Pratt — in his *A Voice
of Warning,* the most influential evangelical piece of the first period
of Mormonism, in a parallel "Contrast between the Doctrine of
Christ and the False Doctrines of the Nineteenth Century" —
placed in contrast to "Be ye therefore perfect, even as your Father
which is in heaven is perfect," his version of "the doctrine of
men": "Do not think to be perfect, for it is impossible to live
without sin." In an 1862 sermon (Journal of Discourses, Vol. 9,
p. 305), Brigham Young took issue on this point with the Apostle
Paul. "It is fully proved in all the revelations that God has ever
given to mankind that they naturally love and admire righteousness, justice and truth more than they do evil. It is, however,
universally received by professors of religion as a Scriptural doctrine that man is naturally opposed to God. This is not so. Paul
says, in his Epistle to the Corinthians, 'But the natural man
receiveth not the things of God,' but I say it is the unnatural 'man
that receiveth not the things of God . . .' The natural man is of
God."

14. On Salvation by Grace

THAT SALVATION IS BY GRACE rather than merit is
entirely consonant with the classical doctrine of original sin.
The doctrine of grace assumed its most extreme form in associa-

tion with the Augustinian-Calvinistic belief in depravity and the loss of full moral freedom, but was somewhat more moderate when conjoined with the Catholic conception of the fall and of free will. Thus the *Westminster Confession of Faith* in 1647, following the general Augustinian pattern of Reformation theology that was grounded in *Ephesians* 2:8, 9: "Those whom God effectually calleth he also freely justifieth; not by infusing righteousness into them, but by pardoning their sins, and by accounting and accepting their persons as righteous; not for any thing wrought in them, or done by them, but for Christ's sake alone. . . . Yet inasmuch as he was given by the Father for them, and his obedience and satisfaction accepted in their stead, and both freely, not for any thing in them, their justification is only of free grace; that both the exact justice and rich grace of God might be glorified in the justification of sinners."[28]

A century earlier, the *Augsburg Confession* of 1530, composed by Melanchthon as a normative statement of Lutheran doctrine, had asserted that ". . . men can not be justified [obtain forgiveness of sins and righteousness] before God by their own powers, merits, or works, but are justified freely [of grace] for Christ's sake through faith, when they believe that they are received into favor, and their sins forgiven for Christ's sake, who by his death hath satisfied for our sins."[29]

In opposition to the general character of the Reformation doctrine of grace, with its insistence that good works are entirely the product of grace and constitute no merit whatsoever for justification, the Council of Trent in 1547 decreed for Catholic theology that "If any one saith, that the good works of one that is justified are in such manner the gifts of God, that they are not also the good merits of him that is justified; or, that the said justified, by the good works which he performs through the grace of God and the merit of Jesus Christ, whose living member he is, does not truly merit increase of grace, eternal life, and the attainment of that eternal life, — if so be, however, that he depart in grace, — and also an increase in glory: let him be anathema."[30]

The Council of Trent here followed the position of the Second Council of Orange in A.D. 529, which had based its pronouncement for the most part on Augustine in opposition to the Pelagian argument that grace is simply an assistance to good works.

Though it recognized merit, the Council of Trent nevertheless supported the Augustinian doctrine of prevenient grace, that an original grace moves the will toward sanctifying faith, a doctrine intimately involved with the belief in predestination and defended by Aquinas, Luther, and Calvin and expounded in the Tenth Article of the Church of England. "The condition of Man after the fall of Adam is such, that he can not turn and prepare himself, by his own natural strength and good works, to faith, and calling upon God. Wherefore we have no power to do good works pleasant and acceptable to God, without the grace of God by Christ preventing us, that we may have a good will, and working with us, when we have that good will."[31] It is the doctrine of prevenient grace, the grace operating on the will to turn it to God, that totally denies to man any merit whatsoever, even the merit of initiating the faith in Christ that brings sanctifying grace. Here Christian orthodoxy took its stand on a principle that guaranteed the utter moral and spiritual impotence of man as a necessary corollary of its absolutistic concept of God.

Mormon theology is not without a doctrine of grace, but it undertakes to conform that doctrine to the belief in merit that is consistent with its denial of original sin and is implicit in its affirmative concept of man. The orthodox position that there is no salvation except by the atonement through Jesus Christ is clearly affirmed. But the atonement, though necessary, is not a sufficient condition for salvation except for those who are not morally accountable, as for instance by reason of their infancy or the fact that they do not live under the law, as in the case of primitives. For all others, the meaning of the atonement is that by the grace of God through Christ it is made possible for man, who is by nature neither corrupt nor depraved, to merit his salvation by free obedience to the law. By the fall man gained the

possibility of a moral life through the implementation of his freedom, and by the atonement he gained the possibility of salvation
in eternal life through merit.

The Mormon doctrine agrees with the traditional theology
that a consequence of the sin of the first man was human mortality. The atonement, therefore, has as a part of its meaning the
restoration of eternal life through the resurrection of Christ. But
if the atonement is to yield more than the resurrection of the body,
as it always has in Christian belief, the fall must entail more
than the loss of immortality. In Mormon theology that "more"
is sometimes described as "spiritual death." It is the state of
being cast out of the presence of the Lord, i.e., banishment from
the garden, but beyond this, "spiritual death" has been difficult
for the Mormon theologians to define and they have usually
passed over it somewhat casually. Yet it needs their careful attention, for it is just here that a bit of the old orthodoxy threatens
to rear its head in the form of something not totally different from
original sin. The eventual treatment of this issue may determine
much of the character of Mormon theology in the future.

At least this much can be said: that, in contrast to the
pattern of Christian theology generally, it is typical of the Mormon
theologians in explication of the doctrine of the fall to concen-
trate primarily on the factor of physical death rather than spiritual
death. And, due especially to their combination of legalism and
literalism, it is not surprising that their description of spiritual
death is sometimes simply the banishment of man from the garden.
(Cf. James E. Talmage, *The Articles of Faith*, p. 67f.) Now,
having the knowledge of good and evil, he is morally free and
morally responsible and is subject to actual sin. But his condition
of exclusion from the divine presence does not in any way constitute sin; he is not by nature sinful, nor does a necessary compul-
sion to actual sin condition his freedom. In what may be considered the classical Mormon theology, nothing is more evident
than the determination to avoid any suggestion that Adam's guilt
can in any way be imputed to mankind. Man suffers the conse-

quence of Adam's transgression in death and estrangement, but
that consequence is not the entailment of sin or guilt. Indeed,
though Adam himself is guilty of transgressing the divine law,
his transgression is not accounted as sinful. To repeat, it is here
in its vigorous denial of original sin that Mormonism takes its
stand in radical opposition to the essential character of traditional
Christianity and, whatever its involvement in the classical theological pattern and in the forms and expressions of fundamentalism, it here exhibits its predominantly liberal character as a
religion that is grounded in a life-affirming positive conception
of the nature of man. For in abandoning the conception of
spiritual death as guilt and sin, the Mormon theologian proceeds
to describe man after the fall in terms of full moral freedom and
all that such freedom entails when considered within the context
of a liberal philosophy concerned with the fulfillment of individual
personality and the progress of society. And as a strange but undis-
guised and quite consistent though paradoxical commitment to
the liberal spirit, the fall itself is declared to conform fully to
the divine will, to be ultimately productive of good rather than
evil. And Adam, rather than incurring the wrath of God, is
described as a moral hero who, discriminating rightly among the
alternatives, wisely brought the possibility of freedom and genuine
morality to the world.

This is a bold and straightforward solution to an age-old
problem posed for Christian theology by its employment of the
story of the fall for doctrinal purposes. What has been aptly called
by Professor Arthur O. Lovejoy the "paradox of the fortunate
fall" has been a perpetual embarrassment to the theologians,
whose absolute God certainly wanted the fall in the first place
or it would not have occurred. Whatever may have been Adam's
sin, without it the whole Christian drama would be meaningless.
Adam's sin was a blessed and a necessary sin, the *felix culpa* of the
Roman liturgy that Milton so dramatically expressed in the words
of Adam in *Paradise Lost*:

> O goodness infinite, goodness immense!
> That all this good of evil shall produce,
> And evil turn to good; more wonderful
> Than that which by creation first brought forth
> Light out of darkness! full of doubt I stand,
> Whether I should repent me now of sin
> By me done or occasion'd, or rejoyce
> Much more, that much more good thereof shall spring,
> To God more glory, more good will to Men
> From God, and over wrauth grace shall abound.[32]

St. Ambrose in the fourth century had explicitly stated that Adam's sin brought more benefit than harm[33] and his contemporary, St. Augustine, who was deeply concerned with the status of Adam's guilt, argued (as has many another Christian theologian since his time) that even evil fulfills the good purposes of God. "The works of God are so wisely and exquisitely contrived that, when an angelic and human creature sins . . . it fulfills what He willed . . . ."

A thousand years later, John Wyclif preached that ". . . alle thingis comen for the beste; for alle comen for Goddis ordenance, and so thei comen for God himself; and so alle thingis that comen fallen for the beste thing that mai be. Moreover, to another witt men seien, that this world is betterid bi everything that fallith therinne, where that it be good or yvel . . . and herfore seith Gregori [St. Gregory], that it was a blesful synne that Adam synnede and his kynde, for bi this the world is beterid; but the ground of this goodnesse stondith in grace of Jesus Christ."[34]

In the seventeenth century St. Francis de Sales declared, "O sin of Adam, truly necessary. . . . Of a truth, we can say with that man of ancient times: 'We should be lost if we had not been lost'; that is to say, our loss has been our gain, since human nature has received more gifts of grace from its redemption by its Savior than it would ever have received from the innocence of Adam, if he had persevered in it. . . ."[35]

The difference, of course, between the Mormon view and that of the more traditional defenders of Adam is that for

Mormon theology, notwithstanding the statements of some Mormon theologians, the good of Adam's transgression lay not primarily in the setting of the stage for the abundant grace of Christ, but in the implementation of the moral freedom of human souls. This is a very great difference and in a sense it epitomizes the central distinction between Mormonism and orthodox Christianity. In the Mormon scripture *The Pearl of Great Price*, after the fall and banishment, Adam is represented as saying, "Blessed be the name of God, for because of my transgression my eyes are opened, and in this life I shall have joy, and again in the flesh I shall see God. And Eve, his wife, heard all these things and was glad, saying: Were it not for our transgression we never should have had seed, and never should have known good and evil, and the joy of our redemption, and the eternal life which God giveth unto all the obedient."[36] Again, there is strong approval in the *Book of Mormon* for Adam's sin (transgression): "Adam fell that men might be; and men are, that they might have joy."[37]

The Mormon theologian encounters difficulties inevitably arising from the retention of a fundamentally orthodox Christology and soteriological pattern, while abandoning the dogma of original sin in terms of which these were structured, and at times he finds refuge in a reminder that both the fall and atonement are, in their detail at least, mysteries that are beyond human comprehension. But there is a basic and dependable consistency, nevertheless, that characterizes the doctrine — that from the denial of original sin there follows a denial of the traditional dogma of salvation by grace only. Although without Christ's atonement there would be no salvation and clearly God through his grace has made salvation available, salvation is the reward for merit, except, as already indicated, for those who do not live under the law, e.g., infants.

Here appears clearly the Pelagian doctrine that salvation comes by obedience to the law as well as by the gospel, a doctrine evidencing the large component of Hebrew religion in Mormon beliefs and attitudes. Consonant with the affirmative doctrine of man, Mormon theological essays abound with the terminology of "merit." Such terms as "good works," "deserve," "reward," and "achievement" are common in the discussion of salvation. Roberts, for instance, asserts the following: "Salvation is a matter of character-building under the Gospel laws and ordinances, and more especially with the direct aid of the Holy Spirit."[38] And again: "Thus by refusing to follow the evil inclinations of the disposition on the one hand, and cultivating noble sentiments on the other, a character may be formed that shall be godlike in its attributes, and consequently its possessor will be fitted to dwell with God, and if so prepared, there is no question but his calling and election are sure."[39]

Compare the optimism of this with the following from Calvin: "What can we expect in the face of God, we miserable ones who are oppressed by such a great load of sins and soiled by an infinite filth, except a very certain confusion such as his indignation brings? Though it fills man with terror and crushes him with despair, yet this thought is necessary for us in order that, being divested of our own righteousness, having given up faith in our own power, being rejected from all expectation of life, we may learn from the understanding of our poverty, misery, and infamy, to prostrate ourselves before the Lord and, by the acknowledgment of our iniquity, powerlessness, and utter ruin, give him all glory of holiness, might, and deliverance."[40]

Jonathan Edwards, the foremost American theologian, who attempted a combination of idealistic metaphysics, Newtonian physics, and Calvinist piety, was fully committed to the concept of God's absolute sovereignty and the predestinarian implication of that doctrine for the nature and predicament of man. God's sovereignty, Edwards admitted, ". . . used to appear like a horrible doctrine to me. But I remember the time very well, when I seemed to be convinced, and fully satisfied, as to the sovereignty of God, and his justice in thus eternally disposing of men, according to his sovereign pleasure. . . . And there has been a wonderful alteration in my mind, with respect to the doctrine of God's sovereignty, from that day to this; so that I scarce ever have found so much as the rising of an objection against it, in the most absolute sense, in God's shewing mercy to whom he will shew mercy, and hardening whom he will. . . . I have often since had not only a conviction, but a delightful conviction. The doctrine has very often appeared exceeding pleasant, bright, and sweet; Absolute sovereignty is what I love to ascribe to God." [41]

In 1731 Edwards' famous sermon "God Glorified in Man's Dependence" set forth the implications for man of the fact of the divine sovereignty, though in a somewhat moderate form in comparison with the position of Calvin himself. Here the glory of God consists in part in the dependence of human souls that issues from their fallen state. "The grace in bestowing this gift [the Son] is great in proportion to our unworthiness to whom it is given; instead of deserving such a gift, we merited infinitely ill of God's hands. . . . Hence those doctrines and schemes of divinity that are in any respect opposite to such an absolute and universal dependence on God, derogate from his glory, and thwart the design of our redemption. . . . However they may allow of a dependence of the redeemed on God, yet they deny a dependence that is so *absolute* and universal. . . . It is by this means that God hath contrived to glorify himself in redemption; and it is fit that he should at least have this glory of those that are the subjects of this redemption, and have the benefit of it. . . . Faith abases men, and exalts God; it gives all the glory of redemption to him alone. It is necessary in order to saving faith, that man should be emptied of himself, be sensible that he is 'wretched, and miserable, and poor, and blind, and naked.' "[42]

Now much of the language and sentiment of Edwards would not appear entirely foreign in a treatise of Mormon doctrine, for the dependence of the soul upon God for its salvation is taken for granted by the pious Mormon. Yet it is the very religion expressed by Edwards against which Mormonism was in part a rebellion, a quality which it shared with numerous intellectual, cultural, and religious movements in the America of the late eighteenth and early nineteenth centuries. The basic difference becomes obvious when one compares the Augustine-Calvin-Edwards doctrine with the remarkably succinct passage in the Mormon scripture *The Pearl of Great Price*: "For behold, this is my work and my glory — to bring to pass the immortality and eternal life of man."[43] The apparent similarity arising from the concept of God's glory is easily misleading. For the Mormon it is not the abject dependence of man in which God finds his glory, nor does his glory consist in the free giving of an unmerited and unearned salvation which he could have withheld. His glory, rather, is in the fact of man's eternal life, which is a supreme value for God and the achievement of which is his major purpose. That this may mean that God's goodness is described not in reference to an arbitrary absolute will but rather as the divine will directing itself to a valued end, where the human soul is the end, does not in the least disturb the Mormon believer and is entirely consonant with the general character of the Mormon theology and religion.

15. On the Freedom of the Will

Nothing in the Mormon conception of man is more in evidence or relates more importantly to the total theological structure than the affirmation of the freedom of the will. Nothing is permitted to compromise that freedom as the essential meaning of personality, whether human or divine, and at every turn of Mormon theological discussion the fact of moral freedom and its implied moral responsibility must be met and accounted for. This is the full freedom of moral choice and moral creativity in which, by a decision genuinely his own, a man stands against God or with him. It is not the freedom of perversity, the freedom to will only evil, that is at times encountered in the traditional theology. It is especially this commitment to the freedom of the will that conditions Mormon theology against the concepts of human depravity, salvation by grace only, divine election, the perseverance of the saints, and every form of predestinationism and stands squarely

against acceptance of the large measure of absolutism characteristic of Christian theology.

In its early formative period Christian philosophy was caught
in a welter of crosscurrents in the matter of the freedom of the
will. Both Hellenistic and Roman culture were greatly affected
by the dogma of fate, by the cyclical conception of human history,
and by the Stoic doctrine of determinism. Even among the
Hebrews, notwithstanding the strong voluntarism that characterized their religion, the case for free will was not entirely clear.
Job is a dramatic affirmation of freedom, and Ecclesiasticus asserts
it in uncompromising terms. According to Josephus the Sadducees
believed in free will while the Essenes denied it. The Pharisees
took a somewhat ambiguous position, but in the *Mishna* the reality
of freedom was championed by the great Rabbi Akiba. The
main problem, of course, was the reconciliation of human freedom
with the power and foreknowledge of God. The Pharisees, especially in the school of Hillel, held that God is to be credited for
everything as a divine providence, yet insisted that men are
responsible for their moral decisions. Akiba wrote: "All is fore-
seen, but freedom is granted."[44]

It was in Philo Judaeus, the chief founder of occidental theistic
philosophy, that the free will problem assumed its characteristic
form, for here were laid the foundations of Christian absolutism
resulting from the conjunction of biblical and rabbinical theology
with the Hellenistic forms of Platonic and Aristotelian metaphysics. The question of free will did not go unnoticed by the
early fathers of the Church, but it was in the work of St. Augustine that the answer for much of Christianity was pounded out.

St. Augustine had vigorously defended the freedom of the will
in philosophical argument, but as a theologian he compromised
that freedom on the ground of his own religious experience and
in conformity to his doctrine of grace. God, in Augustine's theology, is free, but he is unable to sin. The freedom given to man
in Adam, however, ". . . consisted in an ability not to sin [*posse
non peccare*], but also in ability to sin. . . ."[45] In the fall, how-

ever, the ability not to sin was lost, so man, having original sin, has only a partial freedom, the freedom to sin, *non posse non peccare*. It is not possible for him not to sin. In the grace of Christ he has the freedom to sin or not to sin. But in the perpetual sabbath of the eternal felicity of the City of God, when man fulfills his supernatural destiny, he will be like God, unable to sin, *non posse peccare*.[46]

Calvin followed the Augustinian formula in insisting that, although because of the fall man does not have the full freedom of will to choose between good and evil, his choice of evil, nevertheless, is free.

> Man's spirit is so alienated from the justice of God that man conceives, covets, and undertakes nothing that is not evil, perverse, iniquitous, and soiled. Because the heart, totally imbued with the poison of sin, can emit nothing but the fruits of sin. Yet one must not infer therefrom that man sins as constrained by violent necessity. For, man sins with the consent of a very prompt and inclined will. But because man, by the corruption of his affections, very strongly keeps hating the whole righteousness of God and, on the other hand, is fervent in all kinds of evil, it is said that he has not the free power of choosing between good and evil — which is called free will.[47]

The *Westminster Confession* follows Calvin's Augustinian position on the will, declaring that "Man, by his fall into a state of sin, hath wholly lost all ability of will to any spiritual good . . . . [But the converted sinner in the "state of grace" is enabled by God] . . . freely to will and to do that which is spiritually good . . ."[48] while also willing evil. The *Confession* has undergone numerous changes since its enunciation in 1643, but the original of the chapter on free will is unchanged and is still binding on the Presbyterian Church in the United States of America.

It is of interest that Emil Brunner, the celebrated contemporary reform theologian, holds that genuine Christian freedom is "based upon the fact of election. . . . The only true freedom is to know that from all eternity we have been destined, through the Son, for communion with God."[49]

Lutheranism, while condemning the free will doctrine of Pelagianism, was somewhat more moderate than Calvinism, advocating in the *Augsburg Confession*, 1530, for instance, that "man's will hath some liberty to work a civil righteousness, and to choose such things as reason can reach unto . . . [nevertheless, the will] . . . hath no power to work the righteousness of God, or a spiritual righteousness, without the Spirit of God; because that the natural man receiveth not the things of the Spirit of God."[50]

Although in Catholicism the doctrines of grace and original sin are associated with a doctrine of predestination, the freedom of the will has been vigorously defended, both by medieval scholastic philosophy and today's neo-scholasticism. Aquinas argued extensively for free will in both the *Summa Theologica* and the *Summa Contra Gentiles* and the official symbols of the Church are explicit on the subject of freedom. The Council of Trent, for instance, in its sixth session in January 1547, included among the canons on justification the following: "If anyone saith, that, since Adam's sin, the free-will of man is lost and extinguished . . . let him be anathema."[51]

It is fair to say that the general disposition of Christian theology has been in favor of a doctrine of freedom, primarily because of the implication of its denial for the ground of moral responsibility. Conceptions of freedom have differed however, with some arguing that the will must be uncaused if free and others insisting that freedom is compatible with causation. The tendency in some instances to deny the reality of free will has resulted especially from the strong inclination to favor the idea that divine grace and providence entail the concept of predestination if not determinism. Yet efforts have been made even to reconcile free will with belief in predestination. The most impressive work on free will in the entire history of Christian thought, Jonathan Edwards' essay "The Freedom of the Will," is a closely reasoned argument that asserts freedom but denies it as "uncaused cause," insisting in

effect that we are free to will as we please but not free to please
as we please.

In the matter of the free will, the interesting thing about the
Mormon doctrine of the fall is that it is held that not only was
freedom not lost thereby, but, as has already been indicated, that
the fall was necessary to the implementation of genuine moral
freedom. Roberts' description of the positive results of the fall
in this respect is typical: "Meantime, through the Fall, comes our
present state of probation; our opportunities for gaining an experience in this life; of coming in contact with good and evil; learning
to love the one and to despise the other, by seeing them placed
in contrast with each other, working out their respective results,
to the production of happiness on the one hand and misery on
the other — from which experience we shall learn on what basis
rests the eternal felicity of intelligences, and how to perpetuate it
throughout the ages yet unborn."[52] The assumption that man is
characterized essentially by freedom of will is so commonplace
in all Mormon thought that arguments defending the attribution
of free will to man after the fall are virtually unknown in the
literature. Freedom is taken more or less for granted; not simply
the freedom to do evil, but the full freedom of alternative action,
the power of choice between good and evil. The Mormon scriptures abound in references to freedom, the *Book of Mormon*
especially reflecting the Arminian reaction against Calvinistic
determinism. Here there is a general consistency, not only with
the metaphysical doctrine that freedom characterizes the uncreated
intelligences, but also with the denial of the entire catalog of the
fundamentalist dogmas associated with predestination. For as
already indicated, consonant with its commitment to free will,
Mormon theology rejects all forms of predestination and reprobation and repudiates the dogmas of divine election, irresistible
grace, and the perseverance of the saints.

This is not to suggest that the Mormon theologians have contributed to the theory of free will. On the contrary, they have
generally accepted uncritically the common libertarian conception

that defines freedom as the capacity of the self to effect its choice as an uncaused cause. They have made no serious attempt to refine their doctrine or to confront the numerous subtle problems associated with the meaning of freedom within the context of the current analysis of causation and determinism. Indeed, most contemporary Mormon discussion of free will as free moral agency quite commonly confuses it with the various forms of social or political freedom. Here as elsewhere, the Mormon writers of earlier generations enjoyed a more profound grasp of philosophical issues and exhibited greater intellectual acumen in their attempts upon those issues than do their present successors.

16. On the Atonement

WHATEVER JUSTIFICATION there may be for the doctrines of election and predestination in Christian theology derives primarily from the concept of God as the absolute creator of the world and therefore responsible for it in its totality because ultimately it is necessarily determined by his creative act. The denial of creation, taken together with the belief in the uncreated freedom of the self, released Mormon theology from any logical obligation to the doctrine of divine election and its associated concepts and encouraged both the Pelagian and Arminian qualities of the theology and the experimental and pragmatic tendencies of the religion. Indeed, since Mormonism is essentially Pelagian in its theology, exhibiting, as already pointed out, a quite remarkable similarity to the Pelagian doctrines of the fourth and fifth centuries, it is subject to the same criticism and condemnation from orthodoxy that made of Pelagianism the most celebrated heresy in Christian history. But Mormonism outdoes its fifth-century cousin by its denial of the orthodox doctrine of creation, and it thereby produces a basic problem for its own theology in its relation to Christian orthodoxy, the problem of why the doctrine of the salvation of man should involve the traditional pattern of atonement through Christ.

Nevertheless, Mormon theology has with considerable ingenuity constructed its doctrine of salvation around the fall and the atonement, but with radically unorthodox meanings. As already indicated, the fall is described paradoxically as according with the will of God in the interest of creating a context in which human freedom might eventuate in moral achievement. The sacrifice of Christ immediately compensates for the act of Adam, and mankind, who had no part in the act, is free of its negative consequences. The soul is guaranteed immortality — Mormonism is universalistic in this matter — and is released from the condition of spiritual death. Unlike Catholicism, where baptism releases from original sin, or some forms of Protestantism, where the release is by faith or personal commitment, in Mormonism the release from the bad consequences of the fall is fully achieved by Christ's sacrifice and the individual soul is unaffected, therefore, by Adam's transgression. Baptism follows upon faith and repentance and relates to the "actual" sin of the individual. There is, therefore, no infant baptism. But the good consequences of the fall remain. The meaning of the grace of God given through the atonement of Christ is that man by his freedom can now merit salvation. In the atonement the divine grace lifts the burden of the fall, insuring resurrection and immortality to all men and redeeming the individual from his estrangement from God. But that Christ has taken the sins of the world upon himself does not mean, in Mormon theology, that he has by his sinless sacrifice brought the free gift of salvation to mortals steeped in original and actual sin and therefore unworthy of the grace bestowed upon them. In the Mormon doctrine, Christ redeems men from the physical and spiritual death imposed upon them by the transgression of Adam; he overcomes their estrangement which is banishment from the presence of God; but he does not in any way absolve them of the consequences of their own actual evil or save them with high glory in the absence of genuine merit. He forgives. But forgiveness follows repentance.

No facet of Christian theology has been more difficult than the problem of the atonement, the answering of the question why is the salvation of men dependent upon Christ and his death. And

certainly nowhere in Christian theology has there been more
disagreement or greater ambiguity and confusion. The foundations for a doctrine of the atonement are in the New Testament,
and relevant articles can be found even in the Old Testament.
But in the long history of Christian thought the idea of the atonement has reached far beyond its biblical origins to incorporate
elements from popular religion, established legal principles, penal
practices, and common conceptions of justice. The breakdown
of Roman civic institutions and the rise of feudalism, for instance,
inevitably affected the character of this dogma.

Four major conceptions of the atonement can be discerned
in the development of Christian theology, and today the overtones
of all four, together with their language and imagery, are commonplace in the Christian Church. They can be roughly designated
as the substitution, ransom, satisfaction, and moral theories, in
accordance with the order of their historical appearance. Each
can justifiably claim some scriptural support.

The conception of Christ's death as a vicarious expiation of
the sins of men has its roots especially in certain of the theological
statements of the Apostle Paul, as for instance, ". . . our Lord
Jesus Christ, who gave himself for our sins . . ."[53] or "For God
has not destined us for wrath, but to obtain salvation through our
Lord Jesus Christ, who died for us so that whether we wake or
sleep we might live with him."[54] Paul's language indicates that
Christ died "on behalf of" rather than simply "instead of," but
his position, nevertheless, became the ground of the substitution-
ary theory that prevailed widely among the earliest Christian
writers, that Christ was a voluntary sinless sacrifice whose death
satisfied the punishment deserved by sinful men. Here is a strange
coming-together of the sin-offering of the sacrificial cult of the
Jewish temple with the overcoming of the law, a supreme and
ultimate sacrifice of Christ taking upon himself the sin and suffering of mankind in order that men might be justified and reconciled
to the God from whom they are estranged in Adam's sin.

The ransom doctrine, which was to dominate Christian soteriology into the Middle Ages and is even now not an inconsiderable factor in popular religion as well as technical theology, is perhaps best seen in its early form in the second-century theologian, Irenaeus, the first of the Church Fathers to attempt an explicit theory to account for redemption through the death of Christ. The formation of the ransom theory, which has its main scriptural justification in Mark 10:45, was probably the result of the necessity for posing a clear and orderly conception of redemption in opposition to the attractive speculations of Gnosticism. Both Tertullian and Origen contributed to the theory, Tertullian giving the ransom the character of a legal transaction and Origen giving the entire theory something of an ethical quality which it had earlier lacked.

The crux of the ransom theory lies in its concentration on the power and claims of the devil. Because of Adam's sin, according to the theory in its later form, man is under the dominion of the devil and the devil has a claim upon him which God recognizes. The souls of men are purchased from the devil by God who uses Christ as the purchase price or ransom. The devil is deceived into believing that he can retain the soul of Christ after releasing the human souls from their bondage to death. But once the transaction is completed, he loses also the soul of Christ because he cannot keep the soul of divinity in captivity. There is, therefore, a triumph of Christ over the devil and his powers, made possible by God's permitting, in some versions even enticing, the devil to bring about Christ's death, for through his death the souls of men achieve life.

The crude possibilities of the ransom doctrine are exhibited in the account given around the close of the fourth century by Rufinus of Aquileia. "The purpose of the Incarnation . . . was that the divine virtue of the Son of God might be as it were a hook hidden beneath the form of human flesh . . . to lure on the prince of this age to a contest; that the Son might offer him his flesh as a bait and that then the divinity which lay beneath might

catch him and hold him fast with its hook. . . . So he that had
the power of death seized the body of Jesus in death, unaware of
the hook of divinity concealed therein."[55]

Though at the hands of various theologians the ransom theory
varied in detail, the idea that the devil had a right to possess the
souls of men was usually present, explicitly or implicitly, as was
the notion that God had deceived the devil in the transaction by
leading him to believe either that Christ would be one more addi-
tional soul in bondage or that at least the soul of Christ could be
kept in bondage. Over the centuries it was especially these two
ideas, the rights of the devil and the trickery of God, together with
the general crudity of the doctrine representing a kind of legal,
commercial transaction, that made the ransom theory somewhat
unsatisfactory even for those who, like St. Augustine, accepted it.
Often challenged in the East, and denied in the West of course by
the Pelagians, the ransom theory nevertheless generally prevailed
until the twelfth-century Platonist, St. Anselm, the Archbishop
of Canterbury, formulated a more acceptable doctrine on the
basis of the idea of "satisfaction."

St. Anselm's theory, set forth in his brief but immensely important theological treatise *Cur Deus Homo?*, has no place for
the crude notion that the devil has rights which even God must
respect, an idea that had always threatened Christian theology
with the kind of dualism that lies at the base of Manichaeism.
Indeed, in the satisfaction theory of the atonement there is no
place for the devil at all, either with or without rights. The devil
has no rights and, even after the fall, men are properly the
servants of God, not of the devil. The devil himself deserves
nothing but punishment from God.

The atonement in St. Anselm's view is not a conquest of the
devil and of his powers over men. It is, rather, the satisfaction
of the demands imposed by God's own nature, his nature as absolute justice and absolute mercy. Even those who had objected to
the idea that Christ was a ransom paid to the devil had been
unwilling to accept the notion that the death of Christ was de-

manded by God, but Anselm, insisting that the salvation of man
could have been achieved in no other way, argued that the absolute justice of God necessitated that he himself, by becoming
incarnate in Christ, take upon himself the sins of mankind and
through death provide satisfaction for the honor of God that was
lost in the fall of man. Unless satisfaction is given, argued Anselm,
who was influenced by feudal law and feudal conceptions of justice, punishment must follow. And only a divine-human being can
give the satisfaction necessary to the divine honor, for the offense
was infinite and required divinity, and it was at the same time
human, the sin of mankind as a universal in Adam. By his voluntary and undeserved death Christ gained an infinite merit, which,
being sinless, he did not need, but which was needed for the
justification of fallen, sinful man.

Whatever its defects as a theory and whatever its involvement
with medieval attitudes and practices later to be morally outmoded, Anselm's doctrine had the great merit of eliminating the
devil from the discussion of the atonement and placing the whole
matter within the context of the moral problem of divine justice.
This was a major accomplishment and one that has ever since
strongly recommended the satisfaction theory to Christian theologians, both Catholic and Protestant.

The satisfaction theory was central in the soteriology of
Aquinas and the later scholastic theologians, though in Aquinas
especially there were large overtones of ransom imagery and a
strong emphasis on the implications of the atonement for the
moral improvement of man. In the Reformation theologians,
however, due especially to the reaction against scholastic rationalism and to the importance of Augustine to the reformers, the satisfaction theory was severely compromised by strong penal and sub-
stitutionary concepts. For Luther, Christ's assumption of the sins
of men made him sinful and he was, therefore, genuinely a sub-
stitute for sinful men, who were thereby released from their sin.
In the *Commentary on St. Paul's Epistle to the Galatians* Luther
held that "whatsoever sins I, thou, and we all have done, or shall

do hereafter, they are Christ's own sins as verily as if he himself had done them." In taking upon himself the guilt of mankind in order to satisfy it with his own blood, be became "the greatest transgressor, murderer, adulterer, thief, rebel, blasphemer, etc., that ever was or could be in all the world." Such an extreme interpretation of the substitution doctrine reflected Luther's preoccupation with sin, evil, and the struggle with the devil. In Calvin also, but with less exaggeration, the substitution doctrine was central in the concept of the atonement. For both orthodox Lutheranism and Calvinism, the Pauline doctrine of justification by faith only and not by works, either ecclesiastical or moral, was fundamental not only for theology but for religion as well. It was the only doctrine compatible with the firm belief in the corruption of human nature and Christ's voluntary atonement as a substitution for sinful man. "For we are said to be justified through faith," said Calvin, "not in the sense, however, that we receive within us any righteousness, but because the righteousness of Christ is credited to us, entirely as if it were really ours, while our iniquity is not charged to us, so that one can truly call this righteousness simply the remission of sins."[56] In *The Institutes of the Christian Religion* Calvin made the extreme substitution doctrine entirely explicit. "To take away our condemnation, it was not enough for him to suffer any kind of death: to make satisfaction for our redemption a form of death had to be chosen in which he might free us both by transferring our condemnation to himself and by taking our guilt upon himself. . . . he took the role of a guilty man and evildoer."[57] And further: "This is our acquittal: the guilt that held us liable for punishment has been transferred to the head of the Son of God. . . . We must, above all, remember this substitution, lest we tremble and remain anxious throughout life — as if God's righteous vengeance, which the Son of God has taken upon himself, still hung over us."[58]

Mormonism reflects in its doctrine of the atonement the eclecticism that might be expected in a theology that is at once

the inheritor of traditional views and a participant in the reaction against them. It exhibits especially the moralistic interpretation of the atonement that became a hallmark of nineteenth-century liberalism and was a continuation of the heretical doctrine of Abelard in the twelfth century. Abelard had denied the entire substitution-ransom-satisfaction framework and held simply that Christ's voluntary sacrifice moves sinful man to a consciousness of guilt and so to repentance and a moral change of life. "I think therefore," he said in a statement condemned in 1141 by the Council of Sens, "that the purpose and cause of the Incarnation was that He might illuminate the world by His wisdom and excite it to the love of Himself."[59]

The moral impact of Christ's sacrifice upon the sinner had always been an important factor in the doctrine of the atonement, although never before Abelard had it been made central, even though there was scriptural backing for such an interpretation. It was generally found attractive by the scholastics who, as with Aquinas, combined it with the concept of satisfaction, and it was held by the Socinians, who denied any objective saving efficacy to the death of Christ. But not until the nineteenth century did Abelard's heresy produce its full impact. The idea that God's forgiveness is possible only because man, moved by the sacrifice of Christ, repents and overcomes his sin and thereby eliminates the demand for punishment became then a somewhat common element of dissident and liberal theology.

James E. Talmage, whose writings are the most influential on current Mormon thought, and whose theology is extremely legalistic and literalistic, combines the substitution and ransom doctrines in an atonement concept that conceives the death of Christ as a vicarious sacrifice of which the "symbolism of the immolating of animals"[60] is a prototype. Christ's sacrifice was voluntary and love inspired and foreordained in anticipation of the fall. But although for Talmage Christ's death was "a propitiation for broken law, whereby Justice could be fully satisfied, and Mercy be left free to exercise her beneficent influence over the souls of mankind," [61] he held that "The Atonement to be wrought by Jesus the Christ was ordained to overcome death and to provide a means of ransom from the power of Satan."[62] Here in the work of one man is a confused combination of the entire gamut of atonement theories — Christ's blood spilled because God wants sacrifice for sin, to purchase souls from the devil, and to free mercy from the demands of justice.

But the most important facet of the Mormon conception of the atonement, and one to which Talmage gives much attention, is expressed as one of the Articles of Faith written by Joseph Smith: "We believe that through the Atonement of Christ, all mankind may be saved, by obedience to the laws and ordinances of the Gospel." Here is a clear statement that, though the atonement is necessary, salvation is earned. Though the atonement brings immortality and resurrection to all men, salvation is a matter of degree, and the degree attained is a consequence of merit. Every man must answer for his own sins and salvation can come only through obedience to law. Here is the opposite pole from Luther's justification by faith only. As it is said in Hebrews, Christ "became the source of eternal salvation to all who obey him."[63]

The finest passage on the atonement in Mormon literature appears in the *Book of Mormon* itself, a statement that exhibits the main ingredients of Anselm's satisfaction theory. "And thus we see," it reads in part, "that all mankind were fallen, and they were in the grasp of justice; yea, the justice of God, which consigned them forever to be cut off from his presence. And now, the plan of mercy could not be brought about except an atonement should be made; therefore God himself atoneth for the sins of the world, to bring about the plan of mercy, to appease the demands of justice, that God might be a perfect, just God, and a merciful God also."[64] Here there is no element of sacrificial rite, no ransom paid to the devil, no effort to assemble in one formula ideas that, however much they may enjoy the support of scripture and tradition, do not belong together.

PART FOUR

MORMON THEOLOGY AND THE PROBLEM OF EVIL

17. On Evil in the Christian Tradition

IT IS IN THE EXPLANATION of moral and natural evil, the most persistent problem with which theistic philosophy must contend, that Mormon theology exhibits its chief theoretic strength. It is a strength that has never been fully exploited, however, for here again the Mormon theologians generally seem to be unaware of this advantage that accrues from the radically unorthodox character of their primary philosophical commitments. Here the concept of the free will of the uncreated self joins the non-absolutistic conception of the divine power to absolve God of any complicity in the world's moral evil, the evil that is done by men. And the uncreated impersonal environment of God provides the explanation of natural evil, the evils of the world that are not the product of an evil personal will.

The classical Christian theodicy was constructed primarily on the Augustinian doctrine that evil is a privation of the good and has therefore only a negative reality. Evil in no way impugns the divine goodness, since it is not a part of God's creation but rather is the absence of his creativity. This doctrine, which obtains even today in Catholic theology, was occasioned in part at least by the necessity for protecting the accepted theses on the absoluteness of

God's power and goodness. It was in large measure a product of the Platonic identification of degrees of value with degrees of reality, which supported the thesis that matter is evil or is the source of evil, a concept not uncommon in the Hellenistic and Roman worlds. When taken together with the Platonic concept of matter as non-being, this identification of matter and evil encouraged the denial of the positive reality of evil. As exhibited in Plotinus, the foremost Neoplatonist and the chief influence upon Christianity from among the Roman philosophers, this meant a denial of evil not only as a force or power, in contrast to Manichaeism, but even as a positive factor in human experience. Here the Neoplatonic theory of reality as emanations from the Absolute, the One, on the analogy of the diffusion of light from the sun, provided Christian theology with a convenient and attractive interpretation of evil. As the darkness is the absence of light, evil is the absence of the creativity of the divine will. It is in no way a product of that will.

In the seventh book of *The Confessions*, St. Augustine, tortured by his own sins and by the moral corruptions of his world, and determined to contravene the dualism of Manichaeism, eloquently posed the problem of evil:

> And I said, Behold God, and behold what God hath created; and God is good, most mightily and incomparably better than all these; but yet He, who is good, hath created them good, and behold how He encircleth and filleth them. Where, then, is evil, and whence, and how crept it in hither? What is its root, and what its seed? Or has it no being at all? Why, then, do we fear and shun that which has no being? . . . Whence, therefore, is it, seeing that God, who is good, has made all these things good? He, indeed, the greatest and chiefest Good, has created these lesser goods; but both Creator and created are all good. Whence is evil? Or was there some evil matter of which He made and formed and ordered it, but left something in it which He did not convert into good? But why was this? Was He powerless to change the whole lump, so that no evil should remain in it, seeing that He is omnipotent?

Lastly, why would He make anything at all of it, and not rather by the same omnipotency cause it not to be at all? Or could it indeed exist contrary to His will? Or if it were from eternity, why did He permit it so to be for infinite spaces of time in the past, and was pleased so long after to make something out of it?[1]

In *The City of God*, still contending against the Manichees and defending the divine absoluteness, Augustine answered his own searching questions: "Let no one, therefore, look for an efficient cause of the evil will; for it is not efficient, but deficient, as the will itself is not an effecting of something, but a defect. For defection from that which supremely is, to that which has less of being — this is to begin to have an evil will. Now, to seek to discover the causes of these defections — causes, as I have said, not efficient, but deficient — is as if some one sought to see darkness, or hear silence. Yet both of these are known by us, and the former by means only of the eye, the latter only by the ear; but not by their positive actuality, but by their want of it."[2]

St. Thomas Aquinas, greatly influenced here as elsewhere by St. Augustine, continued the privative definition of evil: "Now it is in this that evil consists, namely, in the fact that a thing fails in goodness."[3] "Evil precisely as such," he said further, "is not a reality in things, but a deprivation of some particular good inhering in a particular good."[4] On the question whether God, who is infinite in power and the cause of all that exists, is the cause of evil, as indicated in Isaiah 45:7, he quotes with approval the saying of Augustine that "God is not the author of evil, because He is not the cause of tending to non-being."[5]

There was in the Protestantism of the Reformation a somewhat more positive conception of moral evil that was related theoretically to the conception of positive depravity in the doctrine of original sin and was expressed practically in an intensification of the sense of sin. The Protestant theologians, however, did not produce a constructive theodicy, but rather were inclined to assume that natural evil fulfills an eventually good purpose in the divine economy. They were disposed to satisfy the problem of evil generally by a pious deference to the unknowable and unchallengeable will of God. The absoluteness of the divine sovereignty encouraged some of the less cautious to hazard the possibility that God himself may actually be responsible for man's moral evil. Encouragement for such a belief was found, for instance, in the supralapsarian doctrine of some Calvinists, that God decreed the election and non-election of individual souls even before the fall of Adam. Jacob Arminius specifically charged in 1603 that the Calvinist doctrine of predestination made God the author of sin by an arbitrary decree of reprobation, a criticism expressed also in the decrees of the Council of Trent. This extreme doctrine lost ground at the Synod of Dort even though the supralapsarian doctrine was confirmed. Included among the canons of the Synod was the assertion that the doctrine of divine reprobation, predestination to damnation, "by no means makes God the author of sin (the very thought of which is blasphemy), but declares him to be an awful, irreprehensible, and righteous judge and avenger."[6]

With the rise of religious criticism the easy, naive explanation of evil in terms of the wrath of God, or as otherwise fulfilling the divine purpose, yielded on the one hand to numerous efforts to construct a satisfactory theodicy while preserving the essential absoluteness of God, and on the other hand to a growing skepticism that denied the possibility of a rational theology. The classic expression of this denial, David Hume's *Dialogues Concerning Natural Religion*, insisted unequivocally that from the facts of the world known to human experience, a world filled with misery and pain, it is not possible to argue the existence of an all-powerful benevolent creator. "But there is no view of human life or of the condition of mankind from which, without the greatest violence, we can infer the moral attributes or learn that infinite benevolence, conjoined with infinite power and infinite wisdom, which we must discover by the eyes of faith alone."[7]

But if the skepticism of Hume and the Enlightenment generally was not a full denial of theism, it was at least a decisive rejection of orthodoxy and it was historically a major source of the religious liberalism of the nineteenth century and the naturalistic humanism of the twentieth. Naturalism, of course, in denying the reality of God, escaped all theological inhibitions to a full recognition of the reality of evil as a positive factor in human experience. Protestant liberalism, however, which sometimes became involved in an almost obsessive concern with evil, especially as a fact of the social process, was inevitably immersed in the task of theodicy and, being unwilling to employ the devices of orthodoxy in the protection of theological absolutism, was eventually brought to a tempting flirtation with the heresy of the finitistic concept of God.

As already indicated, the finitism of William James, the most celebrated of modern denials of orthodox absolutism, was integral to his general critique of Hegelian absolutism with its pantheistic inclinations. In large part the entire critique was grounded in a stubborn refusal to deny the claims that the human experience of moral and natural evil makes upon metaphysical and theological speculation. That evil, insisted James, is not to be written off by any technique of negative definition, nor is it to be brushed aside by the demands of faith and piety. If the absolutistic conceptions of God cannot be reconciled with the positive reality of evil, so much the worse for those conceptions. If there is an absolutely good God who is properly an object of religious devotion, he must be a God who is actively involved in the destruction of evil to the limit of his power. Evil, therefore, must be accounted for in terms of an environment over which the divine will does not enjoy absolute dominion.

American personalistic idealism, from which American liberal Protestantism has drawn inspiration for more than half a century, attempted to satisfy the problem of evil without a total departure from the absolutism that it inherited from Hegelianism. The dominant personalistic position expressed by Ralph Tyler Flewelling, for instance, is that in his primary activity, the creation of living personality, God freely imposes limitations upon himself that, like James's environment, provide the explanation of evil. Perhaps less attractive but certainly more radical as a compromise with absolutism is the thesis advanced by Edgar S. Brightman, again avoiding the traditionally distasteful theory of an external environment, that the divine will is conditioned by nonrational factors that are internal to the very nature of God. These factors are the source of evil and he progressively brings them under rational control. Here God is described as "finite-infinite," finite in the power of his will but infinite in goodness and love.

The rise of neoorthodoxy in the decades since World War I has been more than anything else an intensification of theological concern for evil as the product of the sinful perversion of the individual will and as the social consequence of a demonic factor in human history. This intensification is associated generally with a renascence of the Calvinist doctrine of the absolute sovereignty of God. As with typical reformation theology, the inscrutable character of the divine will is assumed to obviate the development of a constructive theodicy. The fact of natural evil is left without explanation.

18. On Evil and Mormon Finitism

IN MORMON THOUGHT evil is seen as a positive factor in the natural world and in human experience, and the primary meaning of human existence is found in the struggle to overcome it. It is a struggle in which the moral decisions of men make a difference, and a very genuine difference, not only in their own destinies, but for the outcome of human history and of the world. The demonic factors, whether moral or natural, are given elements of the world. Moral evil, the evil that men do, is the inevitable consequence of genuine moral freedom. Natural evil, the evil that the world does, results from the moral neutrality of the material universe. God is not ultimately responsible for either that freedom or that neutrality. They are among the elemental uncreated facts of existence. But by entering creatively into human and natural history, God struggles endlessly to extend his dominion over the blind processes of the material world and to cultivate the uses of freedom for the achievement of moral ends.

Mormon literature and Mormon sermons are, of course, replete with the common rationalizations of evil that are more or less standard for theistic religion: that natural or nonmoral evil is a consequence of moral evil, administered by God as either punishment or discipline; that both natural and moral evils are instruments or occasions for the achievement of greater goods, or are partial or incomplete or unrecognized goods; and that evil is a necessary contrast to give meaning and reality to the good, for without evil there could be no good. The one explanation that does not appear in Mormon literature is the complete denial of the reality of evil. All but the first of these have some ground in human experience, and they all enjoy the sanctions of tradition and the support of sacred scripture. Perhaps it is the ready accessibility of these facile but superficial explanations of evil that has so commonly prevented the Mormon theologians from discerning the great theoretical advantage available to a Mormon theodicy by reason of the non-absolutistic character of the Mormon metaphysics and theology.

The most common explanation of evil found in Mormon literature and discussion employs the concept of a dialectical opposition that is grounded in a passage in the *Book of Mormon* which asserts that there must be opposition in all things, including the opposition of good and evil.[8] Now if this is taken to mean that evil exists to make the good possible, as some Mormon writers interpret it, and with good reason, it is at best a questionable concept. For it suggests on the one hand that God either creates or permits evil in the interest of a higher good, and on the other that it is necessary to experience evil to appreciate the good. But few persons responsible for moral education would recommend indulgence in sin as necessary to the cultivation of moral character.

If, however, the passage is taken to mean, as the full intent of the statement seems to justify, not that opposition in all things *must* exist as if for some purpose, but rather simply that it *must* exist in the sense that it inevitably *does* exist, the implications are entirely different. Here is a further justification in Mormon thought for the explanation of evil already described in terms of the non-absolutistic conception of God. But more than that, such an interpretation proposes a fundamental metaphysical concept that has rich theoretic possibilities as a principle of explanation of natural, historical, and cultural phenomena. That reality must be described ultimately in terms of the category of opposition has played a decisive role in the history of metaphysics, appearing with great impact in such diverse places as ancient Taoism, in the early Chinese Yang-Yin doctrine, in pre-Socratic naturalism, especially Heraclitus, in the Hegelian and Marxian dialectic, or in the ontological and cosmological speculations of Whitehead and the metaphysic of history of Arnold Toynbee. Such a conception of things, events, and experience, in terms of an opposition elemental to the very structure of reality, would be of course entirely consonant in Mormon thought with the concept that the world in its most fundamental and ultimate constituents is uncreated, underived, and characterized by dynamic process. It would be inconsonant with a theology committed to an *ex nihilo* doctrine of creation, as St. Augustine so clearly recognized in his polemic against Manichaeism, a doctrine grounded in a metaphysical dualism of good and evil cosmic powers.

Moral evil, the evil that is done by men, has traditionally been explained by moral freedom, the freedom of the will by which, presumably, men determine their own thoughts, attitudes, and actions. That the concept of free will has considerable strength in accounting for moral evil is entirely obvious, but it leaves some crucial matters unresolved, nevertheless, as for instance the severe negative consequences of much moral evil and the extreme nature of some moral temptation. And there is always the great problem resident in the question of the meaning of freedom. For instance: Is a person who chooses an act of crime with *apparent* freedom *genuinely* free to do otherwise if his entire life has been lived within an environment of poverty and sordid behavior?

The freedom of the will, though sometimes theoretically compromised or even denied, has generally been strenuously defended in Judaeo-Christian thought as the necessary ground of moral responsibility. But the classical theologian has always been plagued by the inevitable question of why a God absolute in his power and goodness should create moral wills with the capacity to perpetrate the unspeakable evils of which the human species is capable. Is he not thereby at least indirectly the author of evil as well as good, and even if evil is described negatively as privation, is it not he who is responsible for it, responsible for the limitation of his own creation? The usual answer, of course, has been that it is a great good for God to create persons, and that without moral freedom there can be no genuine personality. Men without the capacity for free decision would be mere automata. The risk of moral evil, therefore, is essential to the achievement of an ultimate good.

Now Mormon theology for the most part follows the traditional pattern in this matter, at least at those points where the tradition supports the full freedom to choose the good as well as evil. And, as in its doctrine of the fall, it makes much of the idea that genuine moral agency is essential to the meaning of personality. But there is in Mormonism a major difference, for in the last analysis the question Why did God create moral freedom? seems not to be appropriate for Mormon theology. It is entirely consistent with the body of Mormon philosophy and theological doctrine to hold that freedom is a property of the uncreated self and that therefore the possibility, even the probability, of moral evil is given in the original structure of things. Moral evil, which is taken as a positive rather than a privative reality, exists not because of God, but in spite of him and notwithstanding his struggle to destroy it.

It is natural evil, however, the evil done by the world to man and to other living things, such as the evils of disease, deformity, flood, famine, or death, that poses the major problem with which a theodicy must contend. For although some concrete evils are occasioned by a composite of moral and natural factors, natural evil belongs to the world which, in the traditional view, God has created as an absolute and omnipotent creator, and for which, therefore, he is totally responsible. The common tendency of orthodox Christianity — a tendency supported at times by the privative theory — has been to declare that such evil is not genuinely real. As with moral evil, it is argued that in some way or another it subserves a higher good, fulfilling the grand purposes of God, and therefore, when seen within the context of the divine economy, as evil it is not *really* real.

As already indicated, a common explanation of natural evil is that it is the consequence of moral evil — a just compensation administered by God for the moral wrongdoing of men. Under such an explanation, so-called natural evil would, of course, not be evil at all. It would be good because it fulfilled a divine and good purpose, the administration of justice. The difficulty with this theory appears obvious. Do men actually find in their own real experiences that natural disaster is related justly to moral wrongdoing? Who is being punished, and for what, when a child is mentally subnormal from birth? Is it really true that those living on the east of a mountain range, where the drought may come, are more wicked than those on the western slopes where the rainfall may be abundant? Or when a tornado strikes does it carefully miss the churches but clean out the saloons? If natural evil is the divine punishment of men, does our experience show that it comes at the right time, to the right persons, and in justifiable amounts?

A second common contention for the unreality of evil is the "blessing-in-disguise" argument. Here there is a partial truth that is taken as the basis for a far-reaching generality. No one will deny that sometimes what appears at close range to be bad turns out in the long run to be good, and that therefore judgment on the value of any actions or events must be careful and considerate and subject to revision. But as a generality, and in its technical form, this position involves much more than appears on the surface. It is the insistence that ultimately evil is not *really* real, that it just appears to be real because of our limited and deficient perspective. If men were capable, so the argument runs, of viewing every event in relation to all others, and if they could see the eventual outcome of what appears now to be misfortune or tragedy, they would realize that all things work toward a good end. In brief, according to this view when pushed to its logical conclusion, the apparent evils are not genuinely evil because they are necessary in the long run to the achievement of the good. If men had the perspective of God they would know that all is for the best.

Now just as some misfortunes are blessings in disguise, it is true also that some clouds have silver linings, and it is certainly true that in the presence of great misfortune or tragedy individuals and societies often and quite heroically cultivate qualities of character and action that are in themselves positive goods. It is well, therefore, to achieve the broadest possible view of things and events. But the question must still be asked: Does this really mean that there are no genuine moral evils in the world? Are not men's supreme tragedies *real* tragedies? Are not some of the pains that they suffer *real* pains? In short, is it not true that after all is said and done men must face the fact of a residue of moral and natural evil that is genuinely real and cannot be reasoned away. And as for the perspective of God, it is in fact a fundamental faith of the Christian tradition that in the incarnation in Christ, God himself entered into the world to take upon himself the sin and suffering of mankind. Is it not reasonable to believe that if God is a compassionate and loving father, he suffers in the real suffering of his children?

It is in pantheism, of course, that the denial of evil achieves its most complete and consistent expression, for if God is identified ontologically with the total reality, the fact of evil would mean that God to that extent is evil. In the usual forms of pantheism there are no distinctions of good and evil. There can be no discrimination whatsoever in a genuine absolute, for by definition the absolute is unconditioned and without relations. Indeed in pantheism, God, who can hardly be conceived as personal but who may achieve the highest expression in human personality, is above all distinctions whatsoever, for he is a total unity that suppresses the determinate character of concrete things and events. From the standpoint of the divine their individuality is lost; it is but an appearance imposed upon finite minds by the limitations of their own perspective and experience. To transcend those limitations of space, time, and understanding, to transcend all finite differentiation, is to discover that all things and all events, whether in themselves they appear to be good or bad, beautiful or ugly, are necessary ingredients of the tranquil harmony of the totality that is God. They should not, and can not, be other than they are.

This doctrine, which is native to both the Orient and the Occident, and with which the Christian Church has at times been tempted, but against which it has nevertheless vigorously defended its theistic theology, is expressed clearly in the *Ethics* of Spinoza, whose pantheistic absolutism is supported by a rigorous logic:

> Nothing in the universe is contingent, but all things are conditioned to exist and operate in a particular manner by the necessity of the divine nature. . . . All things necessarily follow from the nature of God, and by the nature of God are conditioned to exist and act in a particular way. If things, therefore, could have been of a different nature, or have been conditioned to act in a different way, so that the order of nature would have been different, God's nature would also have been able to be different from what it now is.[9]

Mormon theology, grounded as it is in an intensely pluralistic metaphysics, stands at the opposite pole from the pantheism of Spinoza, a pantheism which asserts that all particular realities are but modes of a single unified substance and which consequently denies free will in God and in human personality, insisting that whatever happens, happens necessarily, and that therefore nothing is evil in its ultimate nature. The vocation of man, insisted Spinoza, is to seek a kind of stoic salvation through achieving the understanding that is available to those who see the world *sub specie aeternitatis,* under the aspect of eternity. The attitude of Mormonism toward such a concept is not unlike the polemic of William James against the intellectualistic and pantheistic professions of Hegelian absolutism — that it is proper to man to see the world through his own experience, and seeing it, to refuse to deny what he sees, a world in which pain and suffering, frustration and failure, anguish and death are as real as hope, aspiration, success, happiness, and life. It is a world of incessant struggle to overcome evil, a struggle that is real for God himself, and in which therefore the free moral decisions of men are decisive for their own salvation and govern in part the fulfillment of the divine purpose in human and world history.

Now judged by the classical tradition, it is a radically unorthodox theology that describes God as genuinely involved in a struggle with evil — or to put it crudely, as really playing for keeps. For in the orthodox doctrine, again to put it crudely, he has the whole world in his hand; the whole history of his creation is in his present experience, and he knows the end from the beginning because he determines it by his creative power. Men must struggle with themselves and with their world, but in God there is an eternal peace. Between them there is the infinite ontological distance that separates the creator from the creature. This distance was clearly defined in the first Christian century by Philo Judaeus: "God alone keeps festival in reality, for he alone rejoices, he alone is delighted, he alone feels cheerfulness, and to him alone is it given, to pass an existence of perfect peace unmixed with war. He is free from all pain, and free from all fear; he has no participation in any evils, he yields to no one, he suffers no sorrow, he knows no fatigue, he is full of unalloyed happiness; his nature is entirely perfect, or rather God is himself the perfection, and completion, and boundary of happiness, partaking of nothing else by which he can be rendered better...."[10]

The whole of occidental theology is dominated by this conception of God, which enjoys the support not only of traditional argument but of religious commitment and sentiment as well. Radical departures from it either in doctrine or devotional religion are both difficult and uncommon. But however much it is at times captive to the orthodox rhetoric that rings so majestically from both page and pulpit, and seems so fitting in prayers and devotion, the Mormon theology in its more thoughtful moments disagrees profoundly with Philo and the orthodox tradition, especially at the point of God's transcendence to the world of pain and struggle. Although much that appears to be evil vanishes as knowledge and experience increase, and although often what is thought to be evil proves eventually to be a positive good, there are left those genuine evils, both moral and natural, which cannot be explained away and whose genuineness means that they must be real for God as they are real for man. In Mormon theology God is confronted by evil as intractable fact and it is appropriate to his divine nature to struggle endlessly against it. God is to be found not simply in his heaven, where presumably all is well, but also, to use the language of James, "In this real world of sweat and dirt. . . . His menial services are needed in the dust of our human trials, even more than his dignity is needed in the empyrean."[11]

If St. Augustine were to return and be introduced to modern Christianity through Mormonism, he would be shocked and not a little disappointed to discover that he had not destroyed forever the heresies against which he directed his most vigorous and brilliant intellectual blows. For here he would encounter not only the Pelagianism that he fought so confidently, but also strong indications of the finitism which he identified with the Manichaeism that elicited much of his most intense assault. Here he would find little of the absolutism which in his later years he wrote so securely into the life and structure of Christianity. Nowhere is the denial of this absolutism more evident than in the moralistic conception of the meaning of human existence that dominates so much of Mormon thought and attitude. For although Mormonism as a religion does not cultivate in its adherents the agonized conscience, nor lead them into "the dark night of the soul," it yet forever reminds them that the vocation of man is found in the primary experience of moral struggle and that the God whom they worship participates in that struggle, suffers when they suffer, fails in their failures, grieves for their sins, and rejoices in their triumphs. They are made to believe that they are, as the Apostle said, "laborers together with God," for God has not created evil for some more ultimate purpose, nor the conditions from which it comes, nor does he permit it when he might destroy it.

At least this is Mormonism in those moments when its thought is clear, careful, and consistent with its own primary insights, and when it forcefully exhibits its distinctive character. And here, of course, the religion receives full support from the theology. The thesis that God being conditioned by his own uncreated environment is not absolute in his power reconciles the doctrine of the infinite goodness of God, a belief common to all cultivated theism, with the reality of evil. Clearly the three concepts of the absolute goodness of God, the absoluteness of his power, and the positive reality of evil are not mutually compatible as ingredients of a theistic world view. One of them must be compromised to save the other two. No cultured religion can sacrifice the first; traditional orthodox Christianity has at times lived with inconsistency and at times hesitantly sacrificed the third; Mormonism, much liberal Protestantism, and some philosophical theology have sacrificed the second.

There can be no question of the theoretic strength of a finitistic conception of God in the structure of a theodicy, for it salvages faith in the supreme goodness of God and in the meaningfulness and worth of the moral experience of man. But it would be an error to suppose that Mormonism made the choice for finitism by analyzing the philosophical problem of evil, or that any religion could do so, or that having found its direction, Mormonism has cultivated a non-absolutistic theology consistently and with ease.

On the contrary, the Mormon doctrine that God is finite comes primarily from the unargued pronouncements of Joseph Smith, who appears to have given no direct attention to its implications for the problem of evil, but who propounded it rather as a common sense conception of the nature of the divine personality. And certainly it is a doctrine that does not go unchallenged, especially by those whose thought is careless or undisciplined and who, while professing commitment to Mormonism, fail nevertheless to discern how radically it departs from the foundations of classical Christianity.

The Mormon theologians generally, while assuming the truth of their Prophet's declarations on the relation of God to uncreated selves and the uncreated world, have nevertheless usually followed the thought patterns and terminology characteristic of traditional absolutism in their descriptions of God. They not uncommonly define God as omnipotent, omniscient, and omnipresent, for instance, while at the same time inconsistently defending a form of polytheism and asserting that God has achieved his present status by obedience to law. They have rarely exploited the finitism and temporalism which their philosophy logically demands of them and which provide such a large theoretic advantage in the explanation of the existence of evil. The grip of theological absolutism is not easily broken, for it not only carries the enormous prestige and emotional weight of orthodox religion, and in various ways is supported by rationalistic methodology and the major philosophical tradition, but, perhaps far more importantly, it satisfies the powerful psychological demand for the consolations of religion. Faith in an omnipotent and absolute being holds more appeal than faith in a being who, whatever his powers, does not totally transcend the issues that engross mankind.

It should be observed that Mormon writers frequently employ the terminology of absolutistic theology within non-absolutistic metaphysical contexts. Thus the term "creator" and its cognates mean, when applied to God, that he is the organizer and designer of the world and the sustainer of its forms, but not that he is its creator in the orthodox absolutistic sense; or when God is described as "omnipotent," that omnipotence is compromised necessarily by the other commitments of the theologian. Brigham H. Roberts, for instance, the most vigorous and adventurous of the accepted Mormon theologians, and certainly the most perceptive among them, says that "unless God is regarded as the supreme governing power in the world pertaining to them, men could not center their faith in him for life and salvation. For if the idea existed that his power was not supreme — absolute — fear might be engendered in the hearts of men that there existed still other powers that would overturn his purposes. . . ."[12] Roberts here employs the very term "absolute." But a reading of his own theological works clearly reveals that the expression "pertaining to them" is in deference to the polytheistic thesis that pervades Mormon thought and is intended to set certain limits to the domain of God. The term "absolute" here does not convey the notion of *absolute* absoluteness which it intends in typical technical philosophical and theological discourse. Indeed, more than any other Mormon theologian, Roberts has both discerned and emphasized the finitistic implications of Joseph Smith's teachings and has at times suggested the importance of this finitism for the problem of theodicy. In his essay on Mormonism as a system of philosophy in the official history of the Church, for instance, he is involved repeatedly in this finitism, as in the discussion of God as the Supreme Intelligence in a community of intelligent beings. "Yet to this Supreme Intelligence are the other intelligences necessary. He without them cannot be perfect, nor they without him. There is community of interest between them; also love and brotherhood; and hence community of effort for mutual good, for progress, for attainment of the highest possible." Here is no orthodox absolute God, but one who, whatever his powers, needs the association of others and cooperates with them in the pursuit of ends. Moreover, says Roberts, "the *Absolute Power* over all things," a power yet to be achieved by the community of intelligences, "exists in the harmonized *Will* of all

Divine Intelligences, guided and instructed by the One more intelligent than all — the Eternal God of all other Gods."[13]

In his discussion of evil in a discourse commemorating the one hundred and second anniversary of the Prophet's birth, Roberts described the philosophy of Joseph Smith as holding that moral evil "is not a created thing. It is one of the eternal existences, just as duration is and space. It is as old as law — old as Truth, old as this eternal universe. Intelligences must adjust themselves to these eternal existences . . . ."[14] "Intelligences" in Roberts' discussion includes God as the Superior Intelligence. The terminology is Joseph Smith's. God is not responsible for man's moral evil, insists Roberts, again interpreting the Prophet, for "He creates not their inherent nature; He is not responsible for the use they make of their freedom. . . ."[15] Finally, in the most impressive theological piece to come from an accepted Mormon writer, *The Mormon Doctrine of Deity*, published in 1903 and now virtually forgotten, Roberts expressed clearly the basic argument for finitism in theistic theology: "But we have already seen that God cannot be considered as absolutely infinite, because we are taught by the facts of revelation that absolute infinity cannot hold as to God; as a person, God has limitations, and that which has limitations is not absolutely infinite. If God is conceived of as absolutely infinite, in his substance as in his attributes, then all idea of personality respecting him must be given up; for personality implies limitations."[16]

It is of interest here that the development of the various forms of Vedanta in Hindu philosophy has at times centered on the issue with which Roberts is concerned, whether the absolute (Brahman) can be regarded as a personal God in anything like the sense of occidental theism. Those who have contended in the negative have argued that there can be no genuinely personal absolute because personality entails a distinction between self and not-self. On this ground, the biblical God, who in Christian theology is always set ontologically against his creation, can be considered a person but not an authentic absolute.

Of course, if Mormonism becomes fully articulate philosophically, the numerous problems which inevitably confront a pluralistic metaphysics will arise to plague its theology. In metaphysics, the best explanations inevitably create new problems of their own. Nevertheless, for Mormonism the die of pluralistic metaphysics and finitistic theology is clearly cast, whatever the arguments of the absolutists and whatever the emotions of those Mormon writers who lust after the linguistic fleshpots of orthodoxy.

I love it!

Within the framework of such a theology, it may be held not only that God is not the author of evil, but that evil is genuinely and positively real; that it is real, not just relative to man's limited experience or limited perspective, but is real from any standpoint that may be conceived. And it is possible, moreover, with such theological premises, to believe that God is totally set against all the evils of the world and is committed to their destruction, which destruction is in process as the concomitant production of good is also in process. Within such a theology the absolute goodness of God can be declared while the dignity and creative power and moral responsibility of man are upheld.

This type of theology does not, of course, eliminate all the questions that arise from human experience as men face their daily tasks or the supreme tragedies of their lives. The existence of evil remains a mystery, as the existence of the world itself is a mystery. But the non-absolutistic concept of God affords a foundation for a basic reasoned solution to the theoretical problem of evil and makes it possible at one and the same moment to affirm a faith in an ultimate goodness in the universe while facing squarely the evils that inevitably come upon all men. It is the task of theology and philosophy to attempt the explanation. But it is the task of religion to achieve in men that nobility of character that enables them not only to live through their severest adversity but at times even to accomplish that divine alchemy whereby they transmute loss and sorrow and tragedy into some moral good for the universe.

19. On the Task of Mormon Theology

THE MORMON CONCEPT of man exhibits the affirmative qualities relating to the capacity of human reason and the possibilities of free moral endeavor that characterized Enlightenment thought in the early part of the nineteenth century, that were basic to the liberal Protestantism in the latter part of that century and into the present, and that today lie at the foundations of the typical secular humanism that has issued from American intellectual life. But Mormonism's conception of human possibility far exceeds those of humanism and the standard forms of religious liberalism. Its conception of man is an integral element in the doctrine of cosmic progress that lies at the foundation of both its metaphysics and religion and that informs the general character of all Mormon thought. It is held that, in the forward, upward movement of the world in which God himself is involved, the human soul has infinite possibilities, because in an infinite time through the progressive achievement of knowledge and the mastery of moral will it may not only cultivate in a high degree the finest human qualities, but may even know a measure of perfection that marks the attainment of divinity. Such a doctrine, of course, is an invitation to an easy speculation that some Mormon theologians have been unable to resist — indeed, that they have had no desire to resist. And from it has issued a plethora of ideas that at times are quite irresponsible as serious doctrine. Such ideas are, nevertheless, a frank and ample testimony of the possible reaches of liberal religion when supported by a conception of God that is grounded in the same optimism that nourished the liberal estimate of man.

The primary task of theology is the reconciliation of the revelation to the culture, to make what is taken on faith as the word of God meaningful in the light of accepted science and philosophy. Mormon theology has in the past pursued this task with some consistency and at times with intellectual strength, and certainly with a stubborn independence and indifference to criticism from traditional thought. Today, much of that strength is gone as Mormonism suffers the impact of religious and social conservatism, as the Mormon mind, in the general pattern of contemporary religion, yields to the seductions of irrationalism, and as the energies of the Church are increasingly drained by practical interests.

The most important recent development in occidental religion is the rise of the Christian neoorthodoxy that on a sophisticated level has reestablished the dogma of original sin and the negative conception of man. Although Mormonism has known little of the social and personal failure that has contributed to the success of neoorthodoxy, for the past two decades it has, in common with American and European religion generally, become increasingly conservative in its theology. The most interesting facet of this conservatism is a noticeable tendency, especially in Mormon Church academic circles, to deny the traditional liberalism of Mormon theology by favoring a negative description of human nature and the human predicament. This tendency is more than a criticism of the excessive optimism that has been characteristic of liberalism. It appears to be grounded especially in a strong appetite for traditional orthodoxy that is whetted by a reading of *The Epistle to the Romans* and a taste for those occasional passages like the Mosiah "enemy to God" statement which appear in the Mormon scriptures. And it is aided and abetted by the predilection of the orthodox for whatever demeans humanity for the glory of God. But that Mormonism reflects Christian orthodoxy in its treatment of the Bible, and in its acceptance of many of the dogmas central to traditional Christianity, does not invalidate its essentially liberal character which is defined by its concepts of man and God. A departure from this fundamental liberalism is a departure from the authentic spirit of the Mormon religion.

If it is to satisfy the demand of reasonableness, every theology must today contend with the positivistic critique of metaphysics that denies the meaningfulness of metempirical statements; the naturalistic critique of theism which demands that the natural world of human experience be explained in terms of itself, and the criticism of a modern enlightened moral conscience which refuses to accept the tyranny of antiquated religious forms that are insensitive to the requirement of a genuinely moral and spiritual life. In addition, Christian theology must satisfy the historical criticism that demands the extrication of authentic history from myth and legend, and it must face the scientific judgment that modern culture must inevitably make against philosophies and religions that are committed to now discredited concepts associated with their distant origins. Mormon theology must do all of these and more. It must justify its finitistic theism in a world increasingly divided between absolutists and naturalists, and defend its positive assessment of man and history in a world disenchanted by human failure. It must reconcile its supernaturalism with its own naturalistic and humanistic propensities and defend its belief in revelation in a world grown skeptical and sophisticated in the ways of knowing. It must contend with its own body of myth and legend and with its own provincialism and intense literalism and legalism.

Mormon theology is young and unsophisticated and is not overencumbered with creeds and official pronouncements. Its structure has been virtually untouched by serious and competent effort to achieve internal consistency or exact definition. Yesterday it was vigorous, prophetic, and creative; today it is timid and academic and prefers scholastic rationalization to the adventure of ideas. It is in great need of a definition of the relation of reason to revelation that will preserve the intellectual integrity of the Mormon people and encourage them in an honest and courageous pursuit of truth. It needs a conception of religion in history which will conform to the profound Mormon insight into the dynamic character of all things and thereby release the Mormon religion from the tyranny of the past. And it needs and deserves a new appreciation of the strength of those very heresies in the concepts of God and man that must inevitably make of it an offense to the traditional faith but which are the chief sources of its strength and should already have released it from its bondage to orthodoxy.

But wherever the Mormon theologian turns and to whatever tasks, for a long time to come he must work within the difficult but interesting context of a body of thought and attitude that is a unique and uneasy union of nineteenth-century liberalism with fourth-century Christian fundamentalism.

PART FIVE

THESES ON THE
IDEA THAT GOD IS A PERSON

(Supplementary Essay)

20. *On God as Philosophical Explanation*

THE QUESTION of whether God is a person would seem to require a consideration of the several contexts in which the concept of God is found. There are at least three: (1) the idea of God employed as a metaphysical explanation of the world of our experience; (2) God conceived as the sanction of value; and (3) God as the supreme object of religious devotion and worship. In typical theistic philosophy, of course, all of these are identified and an argument for one is taken as an argument for all. It is assumed that, if there is a God whose existence and nature in some way explain the existence of the world, he is also the ground of moral and other value and the God of religious worship. St. Thomas Aquinas, at the close of his famous argument for the existence of God as the first cause of all motion, concludes, "Therefore it is necessary to arrive at a first mover, moved by no other; and this everyone understands to be God." [1]

Now it seems to me that if St. Thomas means by "everyone" theologians and metaphysicians like himself, he may be quite right. But if everyone is really everyone, the rank and file of believers in

God, they do not understand that he is a First Mover, or a First Efficient Cause. They understand that he is a just and compassionate Father who rejoices in their joys and suffers in their sufferings, who is the ground of their being and the refuge of their souls.

My thesis is a very simple one: That the philosopher's God, who is the explanation of the world, need not be a person; and the sanction of moral virtue need not be a personal God; but that the God of religion is a person; that, if there is a personal God, religion as it has been known to us in Western culture is true. But if not, to borrow the words of Professor William Pepperell Montague, "the voice of God which has so often been heard" is nothing more than "man's own cry mockingly echoed back to him by the encompassing void."[2]

Historically, the most impressive attempt to provide a philosophical explanation for the processes of the natural world is the metaphysics of Aristotle. God is the eternal, immutable, and necessarily existent first and final cause, the unmoved mover of the world. "We say," said Aristotle, "that God is a living being, eternal, most good, so that life and duration continuous and eternal belong to God; for this *is* God."[3] But Aristotle's God, though a real being and not simply ideal or an abstraction, is not in any sense a person. He is a thinking being; indeed he is pure thought — but pure thought thinking only itself. He is pure act, but is active only as contemplation. He moves the world, but only because it is attracted to him. He sustains the processes of the world, but he does not know that the world exists. You and I are dependent upon him, but he is not aware of us. He is without concern and without compassion. He knows nothing of human history or human tragedy. He is unaware of our hopes or aspirations and hears no cries of pain or suffering. No prayers can reach him, no devotion or worship touch him. For Aristotle God is not a person. His is the classic form of impersonalistic theology. It is with good reason that Whitehead said of Aristotle's metaphysics:

"It did not lead him very far towards the production of a God available for religious purposes."[4]

Now if we cast about for a metaphysic that undertakes to accomplish the task which Aristotle set for himself, to provide an explanation for the world, and in doing so describe the ultimate being as in essential nature personal, perhaps the most interesting examples are found in the German-born idealism of the last century, especially as it infected British and more particularly American thought into the present century. Indeed, the American forms of personalistic idealism, developed within the general framework of Protestant religious culture and set forth by Josiah Royce and Borden Parker Bowne and their students, are the most effective attempt to reconcile the classical metaphysics to the biblical personalistic theology.

Idealistic metaphysics describes reality essentially in terms of mind and the product of mind, so, although it is not necessarily theistic in character, the possibility of its establishing favorable alliances with theistic religion are entirely obvious. Bowne's meta-physics typically sets the idealistic conception of reality in clear opposition to both materialism and mechanism as these were widely argued at the close of the nineteenth century, claiming the support of both the physical and biological sciences. But, although to deny mechanistic materialism does not in itself establish the case for religion, Bowne assembles an impressive argument from logic, metaphysics, and the theory of knowledge and value that the world ground, the ground of all being, is personal, insisting that on any other terms it is impossible to account for the paradoxical facts that the world is both a unity and a multiplicity, and both identical with itself and in process. Intelligent personality, he held, is the only possible key to the nature of reality in all its diversity of fact and value. "Being, causality, unity, identity," he says in his *Metaphysics*, turn out to be "unintelligible and im-possible apart from intelligence. . . . Living, acting intelligence is the source of all truth and reality, and is its own and only stand-ard."[5]

I have mentioned Aristotle's metaphysics and American personalistic idealism, not because of any conviction that either is in principle a true description of reality, but rather because here are two systems of metaphysics similar in intent and purpose and not entirely unlike in substance, where one settles for an impersonal conception of the ground of the world and the other insists that the very nature even of impersonal reality is unthinkable unless personality lies at its foundation. It can be argued, of course, and I think somewhat justifiably, that Royce, Bowne, and others among the idealists, or outside of idealism for that matter, were engaged in a subtle and sophisticated, but not-too-well-disguised rationalization of the personal conception of God inherited by Christianity from the Hebrew biblical religion. The fact remains, however, that their position is not a dogmatic one, but is argued, and argued brilliantly.

The problem we face, of course, is whether there is any reliable method for assessing the adequacy and truth of a thesis in metaphysics, whether we can choose between Aristotle and Bowne at the point in issue, or for that matter decide for any basic philosophical claim. The problem of personalism versus impersonalism is complicated by many factors, as exhibited for instance in the stubborn position of no less a mind than the Oxford philosopher F. H. Bradley, the foremost of the British idealists, who argued that God or the Absolute cannot be conceived as personal, but must be superpersonal. "If the term 'personal,' " says Bradley in his *Appearance and Reality*, "is to bear anything like its ordinary sense, assuredly the Absolute is not merely personal. It is not personal, because it is personal and more. It is, in a word, super-personal." But "it is better to affirm personality than to call the Absolute impersonal. But neither mistake should be necessary. The Absolute stands above, and not below, its internal distinctions."[6] For God to be a person, insists Bradley, he would have to be finite. But that's another story.

With regard to the question of deciding among competent systems of metaphysics, as those of Aristotle, Bowne, and Bradley,

I can only express my own strong skeptical prejudice that is rooted in a reliance on the dictates of experience and a suspicion of speculation, however closely and ingeniously reasoned. It seems to me that we have no reliable ground on which to decide among them, that therefore if the question whether God is a person must be answered simply by resort to rational metaphysics, there is no possibility of our resolving it. I do not mean by this to suggest that, of several arguments, one may not be more logical, or exhibit more insight or perceptiveness, or be grounded more adequately or faithfully in fact or on acceptable scientific theory. My reservations rest rather on the conviction that, when tested by rigorous empirical criteria of meaningfulness, much of the content of metaphysics, including theology, proves to be quite meaningless, however interesting and attractive, and that the meaningful remainder, such as it may be, is so highly speculative that even if we come out of the ordeal with the truth we nevertheless have no way of knowing that it is the truth.

21. On God as Moral Ground and Sanction

BUT BEFORE TURNING to the issue of God as the sanction of value I must confess to another relevant bias, a naturalistic one, which raises the question whether it is meaningful to look outside nature for explanations of things, events, or processes that are found in nature. The consequences of the naturalistic bias are positive as well as negative, for, though the naturalist denies himself the luxury of such a grand speculation as that there is a supernatural personal force permeating the cosmos, he is deeply conscious of the miracle of the personality that is so obviously part and parcel of nature and than which nothing is more real and which nothing equals in value in the cosmos. Whether the question how it got there is meaningful or not, or if meaningful whether it can be answered or not, it is clearly true that persons are not less solidly built into the structure of things than sticks and stones and the sun, moon, and stars. Naturalism, indeed, is capable of genuine piety, a piety that issues from a reverence of personality and a commitment to whatever is authentically humane.

Now when we raise the question of value and its ground and sanction, the matter is again complicated by the limits of experience, the possibilities of meaninglessness, and the hazards of speculation. It may very well be true that there is a personal God whose mind is the ultimate residence of value and whose will is the moral law by which we live, a God even who rewards us for our virtues and punishes us for our sins. But if it is true, there would seem to be no way by which we can through natural knowledge know that it is true. We cannot argue to this end simply from the fact that we have values, that we make value judgments and value decisions, that we prize some things and despise others. For there is the theoretic possibility that values exist in the very structure of reality, not as the creations of a creator God or a facet of his being, but, as Plato held, as universal entities that are objective, eternal, and impersonal. I personally doubt that this is true, but it is a theory that is not to be judged lightly. Perhaps no idea has had a greater impact upon our culture than the concept of real value universals, that truth, for instance, and beauty, goodness, holiness, piety, justice, and whatever else may be judged as having worth exist in their own right as immutable absolutes that are the ground for aesthetic judgment and moral decision and action. Though occidental theism has commonly conceived these absolutes as sustained, if not created, by the mind and will of God, the doctrine of their reality was well established long before they were fastened upon by the theologians in their effort to reconcile the biblical conception of a personal God with the impersonalistic metaphysics of the Hellenic culture.

But the question of value sanction is much simpler than the issue of the objective reality of values, for in a sense it can be answered from moral experience. It is obvious that in occidental culture, which has been traditionally dominated by theistic religion, the religious sanction for morality, for instance, is very strong. Men act in accordance with what they take to be the will of God, or at least they believe that they should act in accordance with his will. And the religious and theological literature and church creeds describe God as a moral person who prescribes the moral attitudes and conduct for mankind.

Now we would rightly deplore the worship of a God who was not believed to be in some way an embodiment of supreme goodness and concerned for the moral quality of human life. And we would be quite justified in our contempt for any church that failed to enjoin a high morality in its adherents. But the question at issue is whether our commitment to moral values in some way or another does or should depend upon the existence of a personal moral God, or upon belief in such a being, or can be taken as evidence for his existence. It seems to me that, though morality is often made dependent upon religion, so that the will of God is the sanction of moral value, such a dependence is not theoretically necessary and may be most unwise in practice. For we may properly ask what should be the moral conduct of those who have no belief in God. Should they not be devoted to the good life equally with those who are believers? Or what of those whose morality is grounded in religion who abandon their religious beliefs and lose their faith in God. Does this justify their abandonment of moral virtue and logically enjoin upon them a kind of amorality and indifference to all value? Clearly this would be indefensible, for by whatever way we may rationalize our moral motives, we actually seek those things which as human beings we regard as good. We believe, of course, that God wills them, as very well he may, but to disbelieve in God would hardly justify our failure to behave as human beings.

In principle, morality does not require a religious sanction even though there may be those of such depravity that their own motive for good is their concern for divine rewards and punishments. If a man is an atheist he is not for this reason bad. He may in fact be mistaken in his beliefs and the temper of his life may be deeply affected by his atheism, for the tragedy of existence may be more evident to him than to some others. But he may be not only not less but even more devoted to whatever is worthy of human endeavor than one whose reason for moral effort is grounded not so much in humane considerations as in theological beliefs.

Now my point is simply this: that these considerations, on the theoretic possibility of objectively real but impersonal value universals in the Platonic style and on the principle of moral sanction, indicate that the existence of a personal God is not essential to either the theoretic explanation of value or the pursuit of a genuinely moral life. It seems to me that it is no more possible to make a case for traditional personalistic theism on the basis of the argument that God is the necessary ground and sanction for values than by the methods of metaphysical speculation, intended to explain by a theory of reality the world of our experience.

22. On the Living God of Religion

BUT WHEN WE TURN from metaphysics, theology, and morals to the question of religion itself, where God is taken as an object of devotion and worship, of wonder, reverence, and awe, it is quite another matter. I do not mean that there cannot be a religion that is based on an impersonal conception of God, or even a religion that is totally naturalistic or humanistic and dispenses entirely with the idea of God. But religion as it has been known for many centuries, especially in the western world — the Judaic-Christian-Islamic religion that has both its history and substantive roots in the prophetic religion of the ancient Hebrews — is grounded in the belief that there is a living God who is a person and in the faith that the souls of men are central to his purpose. It is a religion that must be defined not simply in terms of a conception of God or of man or of human or cosmic values, but rather as an experiential relation of man to God and God to man; that is, a relation of finite persons to the divine person, of contingent beings to the ground of their being.

In the whole of the Judaic-Christian religion nothing is quite so fundamental as the often-repeated declaration of the scripture that God is a living God, who said to Moses as he stood in dread before the burning bush, "I am who I am," or "I shall be there." This was the living existential God, not the conceptual God of the philosophers and theologians, of whom Isaiah cried "For mine eyes have seen the King, the Lord of hosts," of whom Jeremiah declared, "But the Lord is the true God, he is the living God . . . at his wrath the earth shall tremble, and the nations shall not be able to abide his indignation. . . . He hath made the earth by his power, he hath established the world by his wisdom, and hath stretched out the heavens by his discretion." He is a just God, and merciful and compassionate. But his holiness overwhelms with awe and to swear by the living God is to swear by the God of terror and dread. As it is said in Hebrews 10:31, "It is a fearful thing to fall into the hands of the living God."

This is not the God of the philosophers, however much they may wonder on the mystery of things, for their God is a principle of rational explanation. They know of him but they cannot encounter him. It is not the God of the theologians, for the theologians lay the veneer of their life-destroying intellect over everything they touch. And it is not merely the God of the moral life, though it was the supreme achievement of the Judaic religion that the God who became the God of all mankind was invested with every moral perfection and his sovereign will became the moral law. This is, rather, the God of religion. When we ask the question of whether God is a person, it is here and only here that the crucial issue lies.

Now, that God is a person is a religious belief found throughout the world. Popular religion, of course, everywhere personifies its gods, fashioning them in varying degrees in human form, for even among the most sophisticated the play of concrete imagery commonly accentuates the anthropomorphic elements in religious worship. But personalistic theism as a clearly defined, articulate, and institutionalized position is especially a phenomenon of those religions of Western origin. It has not been unknown in Chinese culture, especially in the instance of Mohism, which flourished for a few generations after the death of its founder, Mo Tzu, in the early fourth century before Christ. The God Shang Ti appears to have been for the Mohists a supreme supernatural personal deity who enjoined a universal love, peace, and civic morality. But Confucianism, of which Mohism was a severe critic and rival, more adequately expressed the humanistic, naturalistic, and pragmatic proclivities of the Chinese mind, and the impersonalistic Taoism satisfied better the Chinese mystic temper when it appeared. Shang Ti as a divine person was no match for T'ien, the impersonal heaven that has dominated most Chinese religion, or the Tao, the nameless eternal absolute that is the harmony of all opposites and the ground of all being.

In India, on the other hand, where personal gods have flourished in profusion, personalistic theism has been often highly developed, as found for instance in the *Bhagavad-Gita*, in the worship of Krishna, the greatest of the incarnations of Vishnu, or in the philosophically sophisticated Vaisnava Vedanta schools whose foremost representative, the eleventh-century philosopher Ramanuja, described God as a divine person, immanent in the world and transcendent to it, a self-conscious being of will and purpose possessing every good quality.

But if Chinese theism was defeated by naturalism and humanism, Indian theism in all its forms has been constantly pressed from below by the ever-present nature polytheism, and from above by the metaphysical monism and absolutism that have a penchant for absorbing and obliterating personality.

Certainly there is no more interesting problem in the historical study of religion than the explanation of the defeat of the divine personality by impersonal absolutes in India, China, or ancient Greece, while it achieved such an overwhelming victory in the religion of the Hebrews, giving that religion a most remarkable vitality by which it conquered much of the world. It seems to me that the personalistic theism which lies at the foundation of occi-

dental religion is causally associated with the *exclusivism* which so
commonly characterizes that religion, and that the impersonalism
that dominates much Eastern religion is related to the *inclusivism*
of the oriental faiths.

The occidental exclusiveness is well known to all of us as a
dominant character of our religious orientation and perspective,
and its impact on religious doctrine is readily evident, though in
a sense, of course, it is preserved and transmitted by the doctrine.
I refer to the common view that there is only one true God, one
and only one body of true doctrine, one and only one true church,
one and only one way by which men can be saved. In varying
ways and degrees this exclusivism permeates Judaism, Christianity,
and Islam, the three Western faiths. In Judaism the symbol is
the command of the Torah, "I am the Lord thy God, thou shalt
have no other gods before me." For Christianity it is the warning
that "There is no other name under heaven by which men can be
saved." And in Islam it is the first principle of the faith that
"there is only one God, Allah, and Mohammed is his prophet."

This attitude of exclusivism, which, while compromised in
countless ways, has far-reaching implications for both theory and
practice, is in marked contrast to the liberal inclusiveness so
common to the Eastern cultures. That extreme ecumenical tendency is exhibited, for instance, in the Chinese practice of San
Chiao where the masses not uncommonly embrace an eclectic
faith compounded of Taoism, Confucianism, and Mahayana
Buddhism, or in the religious complex common in Japan where
there is a remarkable conjunction of Shinto and Buddhism. But
in India, in the great conglomerate of sects, ceremonies, languages,
gods, attitudes, beliefs, and technical philosophies known to us as
Hinduism, there is a most remarkable degree of mutual recognition and accommodation. The relation of this inclusiveness to
the concept of the divine personality is most effectively exhibited
in India and perhaps in Greece, for in the ancient Hellenic religion the gods, who of course were persons, got on famously with
one another in spite of their petty jealousies and warfare. The

point is that no one of the gods was raised up as the only god. No one denied not only the power but the very existence of the others.

There have been, unquestionably, countless interrelated and subtle factors in the life and culture of China, India, Greece or Israel that have determined the relative strength of personalistic and impersonalistic religion and philosophic thought, but it seems to me that among these factors none could be more important than this issue of exclusiveness and inclusiveness. My thesis is simply this, that the biblical exclusiveness produced, or was identified with, the contest of Yahweh against the other deities that in various ways laid claim upon the Hebrew people, and the contest resulted not only in the triumph of Yahweh over the baalim, but in the triumph of personalistic theism over impersonalism. This was a contest, of course, in the minds of men, but it is portrayed with great dramatic force in the biblical account of the movement of the Hebrew religion from its early beginnings to the majestic theism exhibited in the pronouncements of Jeremiah and the exilic and post-exilic prophets. It was a contest of the desert Lord of Hosts with the Egyptian deities of the Hebrew past, with the local divinities of the Canaanite fertility cults, or with the imported baalim of Syria and Phoenicia. It drew its sanction and certainly much of its remarkable energy from the Exodus commandment, "Thou shalt have no other gods before me." Certainly it was inextricably involved with the economic and political issues that in various and subtle ways contribute inevitably to the theology of a people. And it is symbolized for us in the tradition of Elijah's contest with the priests of the Tyrian baal, Melkart, at Mt. Carmel.

Now my point is that this achievement of monotheism with its high ethical character is the story of the God of Sinai who would have no other gods before him, or for that matter beside him, who, to put it crudely, took on all comers in open contest and defeated them, establishing first that they were powerless, as in the Elijah legend, and eventually, as in Jeremiah, that they were figments

of the imagination. In this way the movement of the religion
in the direction of an increasing moral and intellectual refinement
was a movement toward a more clearly defined personalistic conception of God, for as the personal God Yahweh eliminated his
competition he was by his devotees invested with the powers of
the defeated, with the result that be became, as in Job and the
later theology, the God who creates and moves the universe and
who legislates his purposes upon human history, the God whose
status as the ultimate reality was established for occidental religion
by the eventual conquest of the Western world by the biblical
faith.

Compare this with the quite miserable fate of Zeus, an early
Greek contemporary of Yahweh, who at one time enjoyed ascend-
ancy in the Olympian pantheon. But Zeus was a liberal, not given
to solitude, and unlike the God of Sinai he permitted *his* mountain
to become cluttered up with a motley crowd of divinities who indeed fought among themselves in a series of friendly in-family
bouts, but who were nevertheless altogether too congenial, so that
no one took a decisive stand against the others. The result was
inevitable. The movement away from polytheism eventually
passed them by, and they all died. In the heroic monotheism
of the tragic poet Aeschylus, for instance, the name of Zeus remains, but already his personality has largely disappeared in favor
of impersonal cosmic forces. And in Plato and the Platonists,
who were moved by a powerful monistic persuasion, the metaphysical quest for ultimate reality and ultimate value transcended
every consideration of personal deities and produced the impersonal, absolute universals that largely dominated the thought of
late classical antiquity.

Like the Olympian deities, the great Vedic gods of India are
the personifications of natural functions; they exist today because
no one of them has driven the others from the field, and because
the religious culture of the masses is in that borderland that
nourishes polytheism in the presence of high intellectual sophistication. But this does not mean that India has not had or does not

now have a genuine feeling for monism, for quite the opposite is true. Nowhere has the inclination toward unity been more pronounced, or its impact on the metaphysics been more effective. But this is just the point. The generosity of Indian inclusiveness has let the gods dwell happily with one another, while, as in Greece, the monism passed them by. It is found in the sages and philosophers, expressed in impersonalistic descriptions of an ultimate reality. In the Brahman-Atman doctrine of Advaita Vedanta, the most notable of the Indian monistic philosophies, it is identification with this Absolute that releases the self from the finite limitations of selfhood, which is the achievement of the Nirvana that is a transcending of particular personality.

The case of Brahman, incidentally, is highly instructive. Brahman today is the impersonal Absolute, the totality of reality in a sense as viewed externally. But back in the Vedic age Brahma was a personal deity who eventually rose, in the Hindu Trimurti in association with Vishnu and Shiva, to the status of creator, the all-powerful God of the universe. In this position he absorbed numerous local deities, and innumerable temples for his worship were erected. But this was, in a rather strange way, his undoing, for, although he contested with his colleagues for power and status, he did not contest their reality and did not eliminate them, but rather came to terms with them. The powerful monistic thrust of Hindu culture, therefore, changing even the gender of his name, converted him into a neutral impersonal Absolute whose reality was over and above that of the personal gods, who became thereby subordinate and convenient expressions of the Absolute. With a few negligible exceptions the temples to Brahma disappeared and his religion was disestablished. He was received by the philosophers, whose impersonal absolutes transcend the personalistic formulations of sectarianism — all of which is most fortunate for my theory.

The personal concept of God set forth in the Hebrew scriptures is not the result of metaphysical or theological speculation or disputation. It is rather the product of a sense of living involvement with a God who more than anything else is the sovereign of the moral law and the Lord of history. Nothing could have contributed more to the conviction that God is a person, or to the strengthening of that idea and its preservation as the conceptual foundation of religion, than the remarkable and quite unparalleled consciousness of history that pervades the mentality of the Bible. It is a historical sense that deeply infects the whole character of Hebrew and Judaic culture and determines in large measure the quality of both morals and religion and can be seen on virtually every page of the scripture, whether it is poetry or prose, prophecy or wisdom. The genuine reality of history is guaranteed by the temporal nature of God, whose purposes are projected and realized in the course of world events. The world had a beginning and therefore can have an end, so there is a direction and ultimate meaning in human history. It is this meaning that binds God and his purposes so intimately to the world and prevents his loss into the abstractions of the philosophers and theologians. For the Lord of time and history is living and dynamic, with a moral purpose that invades the conscience and decisions of men, instills their hearts with remorse and fear, and impels them to justice and uprightness.

As Judaism and primitive Christianity became increasingly involved with the Graeco-Roman culture of the Mediterranean world, the biblical God triumphed quite handily over the deities of the mystery religions, perhaps more than anything because he was the living embodiment of worth and value and moral will. But the metaphysics of Platonic and Aristotelian origin that permeated Hellenistic thought became a permanent threat to the concept of divine personality. Given the confluence of cultures that were brought together by the Greek and Roman empires, it was inevitable that the biblical religion and the Greek metaphysics should confront one another, and inevitable that they should come to terms with one another to produce a new culture, a new philosophy, and a new religion.

At least three factors in the metaphysics posed problems for the religion as the two combined in Christian theology, as the typical Greek conception of the ultimately real suffused with the Judaeo-Christian divine Father-God. In later centuries they similarly affected Jewish thought. First was the character of the Greek metaphysics, for the philosophers had fashioned impersonal descriptions of reality. For Plato the ultimately real was the universals — the value absolutes, such as truth, beauty, and goodness. And of all the absolutes, the Idea of the Good was the highest and the realest. Not a God who is good, but the Good, timeless, motionless, and impersonal. But the theologians seemed equal to the task. Following the Jewish philosopher Philo Judaeus, some made the personal God the creator of the impersonal absolutes. But for the most part Christian theology has followed St. Augustine, the greatest of the theologians, in placing the absolutes in the mind of God. They are a facet of his very nature. He eternally thinks absolute truth, beauty, goodness, justice, piety, and every value for which there is an experience, and his will conforms to his intellect. In this way, allowing for occasional variations, the theologians protected the personality of God and guaranteed its ontological superiority to every impersonal reality.

But it seems to me that the second problem was not so easily handled. As a matter of fact, though even today the theologians are quite satisfied with the situation, I am inclined to think that they are in difficulties which most of them refuse to recognize. I refer to the problem of time. The ultimately real of typical Greek metaphysics was timeless and changeless. It was the motionless source of motion, the actionless source of action — an impassive, timeless eternal in which there is neither past nor future. These and other descriptions designed originally in the context of an impersonalistic metaphysics became the materials with which the theologians described the living God. They had their reasons, good reasons, for their task was the reconciliation of the revelation of God with the established philosophic cultures. But we face the question of whether it is meaningful to say that there is a person for whom, as St. Thomas says, there is no succession in time, or for whom all things happen simultaneously. Can there be an eternal, nontemporal person? What can be the meaning of personality that is not in time? And what can be the relation to the world of a being which is not in time?

The possible import of this issue becomes more obvious when we examine the third difficulty — the difficulty of absolutism. Can there be an absolute person? Or can the absolute be a person? Now in fact the Christian God is not a genuine absolute, for an absolute in some way embraces the totality of reality. The absolute is unrelated and unconditioned. The only theism that can be genuinely absolutistic is pantheism, the identification of God with everything and everything with God. But in the Christian religion pantheism has always been a heresy. God is not the world. He is its creator. And though he is in it he transcends it, and in his being he is set over against it.

Yet the classical theologians moved the idea of God as far toward the absolute as conscience and reason would allow, and the classical theology is in many ways absolutistic, as evidenced by both the doctrinal and popular concepts of God's infiniteness, his omnipotence, omniscience, and omnipresence. This absolutistic quality is exhibited in any of the established creeds of the Christian churches. An excellent statement is given in the *Westminster Confession of Faith of 1647*. "There is but one only living and true God, who is infinite in being and perfection, a most pure spirit, invisible, without body, parts, or passions, immutable, immense, eternal, incomprehensible, almighty, most wise, most holy, most free, most absolute . . . . God hath all life, glory, goodness, blessedness, in and of himself; and is alone in and unto himself all-sufficient . . . he is the alone foundation of all being, of whom, through whom, and to whom are all things . . . his knowledge is infinite, infallible, and independent upon the creature; so as nothing is to him contingent or uncertain. . . ."

This description of God, which is more or less standard for the great majority of Christianity, is supported by the doctrine of the *ex nihilo* creation, that only God has necessary being, that the totality of the world other than himself, including space and time, is his creation from nothing, created freely and not by necessity, in accordance with his free will and purpose. The question whether it is meaningful to say that God described in these absolutistic terms is a person is, therefore, the question whether God existing as the only reality, without the world, can be conceived to be a person. For under the doctrine, before he created the world God was a person, the totality of reality.

Whether there can be an absolute person is in part, of course, the question: What is a person? The classical definition of "person," grounded in Aristotelian metaphysics, accepted by virtually all medieval philosophers, and basic to the Christian doctrine that God is a person, was given by the sixth-century Roman philosopher Boethius: "A person is an individual substance of a rational nature."[7] St. Thomas Aquinas says, "*Person* signifies what is most perfect in all nature — that is, a subsistent individual of a rational nature. Hence, since everything that is perfect must be attributed to God, forasmuch as His essence contains every perfection, this name *person* is fittingly applied to God, not, however, as it is applied to creatures, but in a more excellent way."[8]

It is generally agreed that an explication of rational nature involves self-consciousness, intellect, and will. These three, at least, are what is meant by a person, whether human or divine, a being conscious of its own being, with the capability of thought, purpose, and act. I will not here press the point of "being acted upon," for though an important consideration, this facet of personality is clearly denied by those theologians and creeds which hold, following Aristotle, that God is without passions, that is, that he is totally active and not passive, that he can affect but not be affected. The God of the theologians has no passions. But the God of religion is compassionate.

Now competent opinion differs widely on the question of an absolute person. It was held, for instance, by the nineteenth-century German philosopher Hermann Lotze, whose arguments underlie much of the technical personalistic metaphysics of the present century, that only the absolute can be personal in the full sense of personality, a view that should endear him to the orthodox theologians. "*Perfect* personality," said Lotze, "is reconcilable only with the conception of an Infinite Being; for finite beings only an approximation to this is attainable."[9]

But the most impressive absolutistic philosopher of the past century, the Oxford idealist F. H. Bradley, insists that it is meaningless to call the Absolute personal. It includes personality, says Bradley, as I have already pointed out, because it includes human persons, and therefore it transcends personality and is superpersonal. But, to quote from his great work *Appearance and Reality*, "The Absolute is not personal, nor is it moral, nor is it beautiful or true. And yet in these denials we may be falling into worse mistakes. For it would be far more incorrect to assert that the Absolute is either false, or ugly, or bad. And it is better to affirm personality than to call the Absolute impersonal. But neither mistake should be necessary. The Absolute stands above, and not below, its internal distinctions. It does not eject them, but it includes them as elements in its fulness."[10]

For the most part, says Bradley, in a passage that all theologians should read, "those who insist on what they call 'the personality of God', are intellectually dishonest. They desire one conclusion, and, to reach it, they argue for another. . . . The Deity, which they want, is of course finite, a person much like themselves, with thoughts and feelings limited and mutable in the process of time. They desire a person in the sense of a self, amongst and over against other selves, moved by personal relations and feelings towards these others — feelings and relations which are altered by the conduct of the others. And, for their purpose, what is not this, is really nothing. . . . Of course for us to ask seriously if the Absolute can be personal in such a way, would be quite absurd. . . . What is not honest is . . . to desire the personality of the Deity in one sense, and then to contend for it in another, and to do one's best to ignore the chasm which separates the two. Once give up

your finite and mutable person, and you have parted with everything which, for you, makes personality important."[11]

Now I personally agree with Bradley. I do not agree with his
own absolutistic metaphysics, but I agree with his analysis of this
problem — that those whose religious faith is faith in a personal
God mean by God as a person something in principle very much
like human finite personality. They do not want to believe that
God is finite. They want him as an infinite person, perfect, without the limitations and imperfections of finite beings. But they
want him, nevertheless, to be a being that, though perfect, is a
self like themselves, having all their own better qualities, though
in perfection. The difficulty encountered is clearly exhibited in
the theologians' contention that God is pure act, without passion.
On philosophical grounds this description of absolute being is not
difficult to justify. The very order of the universe as well as the
perfection of God seems to demand it. But the religious worshipper
cannot tolerate it. His God must be a person with those qualities
that are most valued in finite persons. He must be compassionate;
and the theologians' God cannot with consistency be compassionate. He has no passions. Yet for Christianity the very meaning
of religion is found in the fact of compassion. A religious man may
believe that there is a God who is not compassionate. He may
believe in him, and fear him, and revere him. But he cannot worship him.

It should be obvious that the idea that God is a person derives
from the human experience of human personality. This very fact,
of course, plagues theology with the anthropomorphic, and the
theologians have worked diligently, and I believe quite unsuccess-
fully, to preserve the meaning of personality for the divine while
cleansing it of its multiple anthropomorphic associations and
implications. The celebrated Protestant theologian Karl Barth,
for instance, has argued that the very notion of human personality
derives from the concept of divine personality, a strange and
obviously forced inversion of the obvious. In this way he hopes

to divest the description of God as a person of all anthropomorphisms.

> If we represent to ourselves what this means, it will not
> occur to us to see in this personalizing of the word of God
> a case of anthropomorphism. The problem is not whether
> God is a person but whether we are. Or shall we find
> among us one who in the full and real sense of this concept
> we can call a person? But God is really a person, really a
> free subject.[12]

A major problem is whether it is meaningful to say that
there could be a solitary person, so that God was a person without the world and without any other persons. It is commonly
argued that the very meaning of personality is found only in the
reciprocal relation that obtains between persons, so that the fact
of personality demands the "I-Thou" relation. But in the classical
theology God did not become a person by creating the world.
His nature required no completion. Or is it possible that the theologians are wrong in holding that God does not actually *become*
a person? The philosophers are freer than the theologians, less
inhibited and more adventurous. Martin Buber, with whom we
so commonly associate the idea of the "I-Thou" relationship, holds
that God is the Absolute, but that an absolute personality is a
paradox. Being something of an existentialist and therefore not
one to wince at paradoxes, Buber holds that though one cannot
say that God *is* a person, he can say that God loves as a personality,
for indeed only persons are capable of love.

> God loves as a personality and . . . He wishes to be loved
> like a personality. And if He was not a person in Himself,
> He, so to speak, became one in creating Man, in order to
> love man and be loved by him — in order to love me and
> be loved by me. . . . [The Absolute], though in Himself
> unlimited and unconditioned, lets other beings, limited and
> conditional indeed, exist outside Himself. He even allows
> them to enter into a relation with Him such as seemingly
> can only exist between limited and conditional beings.

This relation is religion. Buber continues:

> It is indeed legitimate to speak of the person of God within the religious relation and in its language; but in so doing we are making no statement about the Absolute which reduces it to the personal. We are rather saying that it enters into the relationship as the Absolute Person whom we call God. One may understand the personality of God as His act. It is, indeed, even permissible for the believer to believe that God became a person for love of him, because in our human mode of existence the only reciprocal relation with us that exists is a personal one.[13]

This remarkably paradoxical and bold idea could come only from a person in whom are joined the unimpassioned reason of the philosopher and the impassioned faith of religious piety.

A somewhat similar position is held by the German-born American philosopher and theologian Paul Tillich, perhaps the foremost theologian of the present time. The personal God of the divine-human encounter, the God of theism, must be transcended to the God above God. For the personal God is a symbol not of being but of *a* being, a being in the world among other beings, a thing among other things, an object among objects. Such a God, says Tillich, is an idol and is used by those who use idol gods in their own interest. God cannot be called a self, for God is not *a* being. Rather he is *Being.* "God is called a person," says Tillich, "but he is a person not in finite separation but in an absolute and unconditional participation in everything. . . . The symbol 'personal God' is absolutely fundamental because an existential relation is a person-to-person relation. Man cannot be ultimately concerned about anything that is less than personal. . . ."[14] But "Personal God" does not mean, he insists, that God is a person. It means, rather, "that God is the ground of everything personal and that he carries within himself the ontological power of personality. He is not a person, but he is not less than personal."[15] He is not *a* being. He does not exist as a thing exists. He is Being, the ground of all existence. Atheism is right, says Tillich, in protesting against God conceived as a personal being who exists.

One final example of a philosopher struggling to accommodate the absolute of rational thought to the personal existential God of religious experience is S. Radhakrishnan, the foremost living philosopher of India, now President of India and formerly professor of philosophy at Oxford University. Radhakrishnan, claiming justification for his metaphysics in the ancient Upanishads, is both a personalistic theist somewhat in the manner of Ramanuja, and an absolute idealist not unlike the eighth-century philosopher Shankara, the chief figure in Vedanta absolutism. The Absolute, insists Radhakrishnan, is not personal. It is the boundless ground of being that is beyond the distinction of personal and impersonal. In the highest mystic experience there is a union with the Absolute, Brahman, a union that transcends personal relationships but does not destroy individual being. But there is another, though lower, experience, the personal confrontation of the personal God of theistic religion. Against his Western critics, who have seen inconsistency and confusion in this dualism, Radhakrishnan has advanced an ingenious argument — God and the Absolute are not ". . . exclusive of each other. The Supreme in its nonrational aspect is the Absolute; in its active aspect it is God."[16]

Now I have cited several examples of the attempt to reconcile in some way the concept of the absolutistic God with the fact of religious experience to exhibit the persistence with which this enterprise is engaged in theology and religious philosophy. But there is, of course, another tradition in occidental religious thought more radical, more adventurous, and far less popular — the abandonment of absolutism and the frank adoption of a finitistic theology. Where finitism has appeared in churched theology it has been readily branded as heresy. Where it has appeared in academic philosophy it has had a tenuous existence as an unstable ground between metaphysical absolutism and naturalistic humanism.

William James, of course, is the most interesting advocate of a finitistic theology. Here was the most brilliant and most ruthless enemy of absolutism in all its forms, the metaphysical absolute, absolutism in moral values, and the absolutistic God. For James the greatest sin was the denial of the obvious testimony of ordinary experience, to submit to the seductions of a speculative reasoning that describes reality in terms not drawn from the concrete facts of life. A conception of God that does not have genuine relevance to the religious and moral experience was for him nothing less than the perpetration of a fraud.

But James's objection to absolutism was on theoretical as well as practical grounds. He was convinced, and I fully agree with his position, that absolutism makes a genuine discrimination between good and evil an impossibility, that an absolutistic conception of God allows no possibility for a theoretical explanation of the existence of evil. Here is the most difficult theoretic problem confronted by the theologians — the reconciliation of the existence of moral and natural evil with the absolute goodness and absolute power of God. The finite conception of God provided an explanation of evil and it made of God a genuinely living person, involved, as James would put it, in the thick of the very work of the world, enhancing its good, destroying its evil in league with man, creating values in a world in which dangers are real and failures are real, but where triumphs also are real and where they make a difference, a difference not only from the perspective of man, but as well from the perspective of God.

Here there is no problem in describing God as a living person, for the materials with which to paint that description are taken from the concrete facts of the most common experience. The finite God of James's philosophy — finite only in power, to make the facts of evil, tragedy, suffering, moral effort, and moral progress meaningful to theology as they are real in experience, but infinite in goodness, if it is infinitely good to suffer in the true sufferings of mankind and rejoice in the happiness and moral achievement of men — that God, described as a genuine person, the champion of every value and filled with love and compassion for mankind, would seem to have great appeal to religion. Here at last is a philosopher who has come to terms with religion as a fact.

But James and the finitistic theologians have failed to capture religion — failed miserably. Even James, the archpluralist and finitist, confessed a mystic's longing for union with the infinite. It is clear that most religionists want an absolute to worship as much as they want a person. Their God must have the whole world in his hand, for they do not propose to take their problems to a God who has problems of his own.

I have failed to even mention mysticism as an approach to the question of whether God is a person. But here there is nothing definitive even if one were to accept as veridical the mystics' accounts of their own experiences. There is always the problem of the impact of philosophical or theological ideas on the very character of the mystic experience. In India mysticism tends toward unity or even complete identification with an impersonal absolute, although the experience of the presence of a personal God is not foreign to Indian mystics. In occidental religion the mystic experience more often is an experience of the person of God. But union with the impersonal absolute is not foreign to Western mystics. The foremost authority on Jewish mysticism, Professor Gershom Scholem, has shown, for instance, that even in Jewish Kabbalism the issue arises of whether the ultimately real, *En-Sof*, is personal or impersonal, impersonal being that becomes personal only in the process of creation.[17]

I do not believe that we can establish by reason whether there is a God, or if there is, whether God is a person. Religion is a matter of faith and hope, or perhaps of mystic experience. It is, to again borrow the words of one of my teachers, Professor Montague, the faith that "what is highest in spirit is also deepest in nature," the faith that the things that matter most are not ultimately at the mercy of the things that matter least. As he has said, it may be that there is no God, that "the existence of all that is beautiful and in any sense good is but the accidental and ineffective by-product of blindly swirling atoms," that we are alone in a world that cares nothing for us or for the values that we create and sustain — that we and they are here for a moment only, and gone, and that eventually there will be left no trace of us in the universe. "A man may well believe that this dreadful thing is true. But only the fool will say in his heart that he is glad that it is true." [18]

WORKS CITED

Part I

1. *The Doctrine and Covenants of the Church of Jesus Christ of Latter-day Saints* (1921 ed.; Salt Lake City: The Church of Jesus Christ of Latter-day Saints, 1935), 93:33.

2. St. Thomas Aquinas, *The "Summa Theologica" of St. Thomas Aquinas*, literally trans. Fathers of the English Dominican Province (London: Burns, Oates, & Washbourne, Ltd., 1920), I, q. 2, a. 3.

3. *Doctrine and Covenants*, 131:7, 8.

4. Orson Pratt (ed.), *The Seer* (Washington, D.C.: Orson Pratt, 1853), Vol. I, No. 2.

5. Joseph Smith, *History of the Church of Jesus Christ of Latter-day Saints, Period I*, Introd. and Notes B. H. Roberts (Salt Lake City: Deseret News, 1905), III, 386.

Part II

1. Justin Martyr, *First Apology*, chap. LIX, trans. M. Dods, *The Writings of Justin Martyr and Athenagoras* ("The Ante-Nicene Christian Library"), eds. Alexander Roberts and James Donaldson (Edinburgh: T & T Clark, 1867), Vol. II.

2. Origen, *De Principiis*, Bk. I, chap. II, sec. 10, trans. Frederick Crombie, *The Writings of Origen* ("The Ante-Nicene Christian Library"), eds. Alexander Roberts and James Donaldson (Edinburgh: T & T Clark, 1878), Vol. X.

3. Moses Maimonides, *Guide for the Perplexed*, trans. M. Friedlander (New York: Hebrew Publishing Company, 1885), Pt. II, chaps. XVI, XXII.

4. St. Thomas Aquinas, *The Summa Theologica*, English Dominican translation, rev. Anton C. Pegis, *Basic Writings of Saint Thomas Aquinas*, ed. Anton C. Pegis (New York: Random House, 1945), I, q. 44, a. 1.

5. *Ibid.*, q. 46, a. 1.

6. *Ibid.*, a. 2.

7. St. Augustine, *Confessions*, trans. J. G. Pilkington, *Basic Writings of St. Augustine*, ed. Whitney J. Oates (New York: Random House, 1948), Bk. XI, chap. V.

8. Karl Barth, *Dogmatics in Outline* (New York: Harper and Row, 1959), p. 55.

9. St. Thomas Aquinas, *The "Summa Theologica" of St. Thomas Aquinas*, literally trans. Fathers of the English Dominican Province (2nd ed.; London: Burns, Oates, & Washbourne, Ltd., 1941), I, q. 118, a. 2.

10. *Ibid.*, a. 3.

11. Frederick R. Tennant, *Philosophical Theology* (Cambridge: Cambridge University Press, 1928), II, 125.

12. Hermann Lotze, *Outlines of the Philosophy of Religion* (Boston: Ginn and Company, 1886), p. 79.

13. Bordon P. Bowne, *Philosophy of Theism* (New York: Harper and Brothers, 1887), p. 191.

14. John Elof Boodin, *God* (New York: Macmillan Co., 1934), p. 145.

15. *Ibid.*, pp. 179 f.

16. Alfred North Whitehead, *Process and Reality* (New York: Macmillan Co., 1941), p. 526.

17. H. Diels, *Fragmente der Vorsokratiker*, Parmenides 8, trans. Kathleen Freeman, *Ancilla to the Pre-Socratic Philosophers* (Oxford: Basil Blackwell, 1948), p. 43f.

18. *Doctrine and Covenants*, 93:33.

19. Joseph Smith, *History of the Church of Jesus Christ of Latter-day Saints, Period I*, Introd. and Notes B. H. Roberts (2nd ed.; Salt Lake City: Deseret News Press, 1950), VI, 308.

20. B. H. Roberts, *A Comprehensive History of the Church of Jesus Christ of Latter-day Saints, Century I* (Salt Lake City: Deseret News Press, 1930), Vol. II, p. 410, n. 56.

21. *The Pearl of Great Price* (1921 ed.; Salt Lake City: The Church of Jesus Christ of Latter-day Saints, 1935), Moses 3:5.

22. Philo Judaeus, *Works of Philo Judaeus*, trans. C. D. Yonge (London: George Bell and Sons, 1890), II, 243.

23. "Dogmatic Constitution on the Catholic Faith," *Dogmatic Decrees of the Vatican Council Concerning the Catholic Faith and the Church of Christ, A.D. 1870*, trans. Archbishop Manning ("The Creeds of Christendom"), ed. Philip Schaff (6th ed.; New York: Harper and Brothers, 1931), II, 239.

24. *The Westminster Confession of Faith, A.D. 1647*, chap. II ("The Creeds of Christendom"), ed. Philip Schaff (New York: Harper and Brothers, 1919), Vol. III.

25. Josiah Royce, *The World and the Individual* (New York: Macmillan Co., 1929), II, 298.

26. William James, *Pragmatism* (New York: Longmans Green & Co., 1946), pp. 290–91.

27. Philo Judaeus, *op. cit.*, pp. 289, 348–49.

28. St. Thomas Aquinas, *The "Summa Theologica" of St. Thomas Aquinas*, literally trans. Fathers of the English Dominican Province (London: Burns, Oates, & Washbourne, Ltd., 1920), I, q. 10, a. 1, 2.

29. St. Thomas Aquinas, *Commentary on Aristotle: On Interpretation*, completed by Cajetan, trans. Jean T. Oesterle (Milwaukee: Marquette University Press, 1962), Bk. I, Lesson XIV, sec. 20.

30. John Calvin, *Institutes of the Christian Religion*, trans. Ford Lewis Battles from the 1559 Latin text (London: SCM Press, Ltd., 1961), Bk. III, chap. XXI, 5.

31. Paul Tillich, *Systematic Theology* (Chicago: University of Chicago Press, 1951), I, 274–76.

32. Alfred North Whitehead, *Adventures of Ideas* (New York: The Macmillan Co., 1933), p. 41.

33. *The Thirty-Nine Articles of Religion of the Church of England*, art. I, American rev. 1801 ("The Creeds of Christendom"), ed. Philip Schaff (6th ed.; New York: Harper and Brothers, 1931), Vol. III.

34. Alfred North Whitehead, *Science and the Modern World* (New York: Macmillan Co., 1927), p. 249.

35. *Loc. cit.*

36. Joseph Smith, *History of the Church of Jesus Christ of Latter-day Saints, Period I*, Introd. and Notes B. H. Roberts (Salt Lake City: Deseret News, 1905), V, 339.

Part III

1. *Doctrine and Covenants*, 93:29.

2. Joseph Smith, *History of the Church of Jesus Christ of Latter-day Saints, Period I*, ed. B. H. Roberts (2nd ed.; Salt Lake City, Deseret News, 1950), VI, 310–12.

3. Origen, *De Principiis*, Bk. III, chap. V, trans. Frederick Crombie, *The Writings of Origen* ("The Ante-Nicene Christian Library"), eds. Alexander Roberts and James Donaldson (Edinburg: T & T Clark, 1878), p. 257.

4. George Holmes Howison, "Human Immortality: Its Positive Argument," *George Holmes Howison: Philosopher and Teacher*, eds. John Wright Buckham and George Malcolm Stratton (Berkeley: University of California Press, 1934), p. 258.

5. From a statement to the *New York Tribune* (Daily Tribune), March 5, 1902; published as Appendix D in G. H. Howison, *The Limits of Evolution and Other Essays* (New York: Macmillan Co., 1904), p. 411.

6. Paul Tillich, *Systematic Theology* (Chicago: University of Chicago Press, 1951), I, 188.

7. *Ibid.*, p. 196.

8. Karl Barth, *Dogmatics in Outline* (New York: Harper and Row, 1959), p. 56.

9. Emil Brunner, *Man in Revolt*, trans. Olive Wyon (London: Lutterworth Press, 1953), p. 90.

10. St. Thomas Aquinas, *The "Summa Theologica" of St. Thomas Aquinas*, literally trans. Fathers of the English Dominican Province (London: Burns, Oates, & Washbourne, Ltd., 1920), I, q. 2, a. 3.

11. Reinhold Niebuhr, *The Nature and Destiny of Man* (New York: Charles Scribner's Sons, 1941), I, 188.

12. Pelagius, *Pro Libero Arbitrio,* quoted by St. Augustine in *On Original Sin,* chap. XIV.

13. Quoted by St. Augustine in *De Gestis Pelagii,* chap. 23.

14. St. Augustine, *De Correptione et Gratia.*

15. John Calvin, *Institutes of the Christian Religion,* trans. Ford Lewis Battles from the 1559 Latin text (London: SCM Press, Ltd., 1961), Bk. II, chap. I, 8.

16. *The Augsburg Confession, A.D. 1530,* Pt. First, art. II, trans. Charles P. Krauth ("The Creeds of Christendom"), ed. Philip Schaff (6th ed.; New York: Harper and Brothers, 1931), Vol. III.

17. *The Thirty-Nine Articles of Religion of the Church of England,* sec. IX ("The Creeds of Christendom"), ed. Philip Schaff, American rev. 1801 (6th ed.; New York: Harper and Brothers, 1931), Vol. III.

18. *The Westminster Confession of Faith, A.D. 1647,* chap. VI, secs. II & III ("The Creeds of Christendom"), ed. Philip Schaff (6th ed.; New York: Harper and Brothers, 1931), Vol. III.

19. Paul Tillich, *Systematic Theology* (Chicago: University of Chicago Press, 1951), II, 56.

20. Emil Brunner, *Dogmatics,* Vol. II, *The Christian Doctrine of Creation and Redemption* (Philadelphia: The Westminster Press, 1952), p. 105.

21. St. Thomas Aquinas, *The "Summa Theologica" of St. Thomas Aquinas,* literally trans. Fathers of the English Dominican Province (London: Burns, Oates, & Washbourne, Ltd., 1920), II, q. 85, a. 2.

22. *The Canons and Dogmatic Decrees of the Council of Trent, A.D. 1563,* Fifth Session, secs. 1 & 2, trans. J. Waterworth ("The Creeds of Christendom"), ed. Philip Schaff (6th ed.; New York: Harper and Brothers, 1931), Vol. II.

23. Brigham Young and Others, *Journal of Discourses* (Liverpool: Brigham Young, June 1867), II, 122.

24. *The Formula of Concord, A.D. 1576*, art. I, negative I, trans. Philip Schaff ("The Creeds of Christendom"), ed. Philip Schaff (6th ed.; New York: Harper and Brothers, 1931), Vol. III.

25. Joseph F. Smith, *Gospel Doctrine* (Salt Lake City: Deseret News, 1919), p. 40, quoted from *Deseret Weekly News*, Vol. XXXIII, pp. 130–31.

26. James E. Talmage, *The Vitality of Mormonism* (Boston: Richard G. Badger, 1919), p. 48.

27. *Ibid.*, p. 45.

28. *The Westminster Confession of Faith, A.D. 1647*, chap. XI, secs. I–III ("The Creeds of Christendom"), ed. Philip Schaff (6th ed.; New York: Harper and Brothers, 1931), Vol. III.

29. *The Augsburg Confession, A.D. 1530*, Pt. First, art. IV, trans. Charles P. Krauth ("The Creeds of Christendom"), ed. Philip Schaff (6th ed.; New York: Harper and Brothers, 1931), Vol. III.

30. *The Canons and Dogmatic Decrees of the Council of Trent, A.D. 1563*, Sixth Sesssion, Canon XXXII, On Justification, trans. J. Waterworth ("The Creeds of Christendom"), ed. Philip Schaff (6th ed.; New York: Harper and Brothers, 1931), Vol. II.

31. *The Thirty-Nine Articles of Religion of the Church of England*, art. X, American rev. 1801 ("The Creeds of Christendom"), ed. Philip Schaff (6th ed.; New York: Harper and Brothers, 1931), Vol. III.

32. John Milton, *Paradise Lost* (New York: The Modern Library, 1950), 12th Bk., lines 469–78.

33. St. Ambrose, *De Institutione Virginis*, chap. 17.

34. Thomas Arnold (ed.), *The Select English Works of John Wyclif* (Oxford: Oxford University Press, 1869), Sermon XC i, pp. 320–21.

35. St. Francis de Sales, *Traite de l'amour de Dieu*.

36. *Pearl of Great Price*, Moses 5:10, 11.

37. *The Book of Mormon* (1950 ed.; Salt Lake City: The Church of Jesus Christ of Latter-day Saints, 1958), II Nephi 2:25.

38. B. H. Roberts, *The Gospel* (7th ed.; Salt Lake City: Deseret Book Co., 1928), p. 208.

39. *Ibid.*, p. 209.

40. John Calvin, "Sin and Death," *Instruction in Faith*, trans. Paul T. Fuhrmann from the 1537 French text (Philadelphia: The Westminster Press, 1949), Sixth essay.

41. Jonathan Edwards, "Conversion of President Edwards," *A Narrative of Many Surprising Conversions in Northampton and Vicinity* (Worcester: Moses W. Grout, 1832), p. 367.

42. Jonathan Edwards, "God Glorified in Man's Dependence," in *The Works of President Edwards, with a Memoir of His Life*, 10 vols., ed. S. E. Dwight (New York, 1929–30).

43. *Pearl of Great Price*, Moses 1:39.

44. Akiba, *Aboth*, chap. III, Mishnah 6, trans. J. Isrelstam ("The Babylonian Talmud"), ed. I. Epstein (London: The Soncino Press, 1935), Pt. IV, Vol. VIII, p. 38. (On the Pharisees, Sadducees, and Essenes cf., Josephus, *Antiquities of the Jews*, Bk. XIII, chap. V, and *Wars of the Jews*, Bk. II, chap. VIII; Louis Finkelstein, *The Pharisees*, Vol. I, chap. XI; and G. F. Moore, *Judaism*, I, 456 ff.)

45. St. Augustine, *The City of God*, Bk. XXII, chap. XXX, trans. M. Dods, *Basic Writings of St. Augustine*, ed. Whitney J. Oates (New York: Random House, 1948).

46. *Ibid.*, Bk. XIV, chaps. X–XIII; Bk. XXII, chap. XXX.

47. John Calvin, *Instruction in Faith*, trans. Paul T. Fuhrmann from the 1537 French text (Philadelphia: The Westminster Press, 1949), Fifth essay.

48. *The Westminster Confession of Faith, A.D. 1647*, chap. IX ("The Creeds of Christendom"), ed. Philip Schaff (6th ed.; New York: Harper and Brothers, 1931), Vol. III.

49. Emil Brunner, *Dogmatics*, Vol. I, *The Christian Doctrine of God* (Philadelphia: The Westminster Press, 1950), p. 313.

50. *The Augsburg Confession, A.D. 1530*, Pt. First, art. XVIII, trans. Charles P. Krauth ("The Creeds of Christendom"), ed. Philip Schaff (6th ed.; Harper and Brothers, 1931), Vol. III.

51. *The Canons and Dogmatic Decrees of the Council of Trent, A.D. 1563*, Sixth Session, chap. XVI, Canon V, trans. J. Waterworth ("The Creeds of Christendom"), ed. Philip Schaff (6th ed.; New York: Harper and Brothers, 1931), Vol. II.

52. B. H. Roberts, *The Gospel* (7th ed.; Salt Lake City: Deseret Book Co., 1928), pp. 27 f.

53. Gal. 1:4.

54. I Thess. 5:9–10.

55. Rufinus of Aquileia, *Commentaries in Symbolum Apostolorum*, pp. 14 f.

56. John Calvin, *Instruction in Faith*, trans. Paul T. Fuhrmann from the 1537 French text (Philadelphia: The Westminster Press, 1949), Sixteenth essay.

57. John Calvin, *Institutes of the Christian Religion*, trans. Ford Lewis Battles from the 1559 Latin text (London: SCM Press, Ltd., 1961), Bk. II, chap. XVI, 5.

58. *Loc. cit.*

59. Pierre Abelard, *Epistle to the Romans* ("Opera"), ed. Cousin, ii, p. 207.

60. James E. Talmage, *A Study of the Articles of Faith* (Salt Lake City: The Church of Jesus Christ of Latter-day Saints, 1941), pp. 77–78.

61. *Ibid.*, p. 76.

62. James E. Talmage, *The Philosophical Basis of Mormonism*, address delivered in San Francisco, 1915 (Salt Lake City: The Church of Jesus Christ of Latter-day Saints, n.d.), p. 10.

63. Heb. 5:9.

64. Alma 42: 14–15.

Part IV

1. St. Augustine, *Confessions*, Bk. VII, chap. V, trans. J. G. Pilkington, *Basic Writings of St. Augustine*, ed. Whitney J. Oates (New York: Random House, 1948).

2. St. Augustine, *The City of God*, Bk. XII, chap. VII, trans. M. Dods, *Basic Writings of St. Augustine*, ed. Whitney J. Oates (New York: Random House, 1948).

3. St. Thomas Aquinas, *The "Summa Theologica" of St. Thomas Aquinas*, literally trans. Fathers of the English Dominican Province (London: Burns, Oates, & Washbourne, Ltd., 1920), I, q. 48, a. 2.

4. St. Thomas Aquinas, *Disputations*, I, de Malo, I, trans. Thomas Gilby, *St. Thomas Aquinas: Philosophical Texts*, ed. Thomas Gilby (London: Oxford University Press, 1956).

5. St. Thomas Aquinas, *The "Summa Theologica" of St. Thomas Aquinas*, literally trans. Fathers of the English Dominican Province (London: Burns, Oates, & Washbourne, Ltd., 1920), I, q. 49, a. 2; Cf. also *Summa Contra Gentiles*, Bk. III, chaps. VII, X.

6. *The Canons of the Synod of Dort*, "First Head of Doctrine," art. XV, the English text from the Constitution of the Reformed Church in America ("The Creeds of Christendom"), ed. Philip Schaff (New York: Harper and Brothers, 1919), Vol. III.

7. David Hume, *Dialogues Concerning Natural Religion* (New York: Hafner Publishing Co., 1948), Pt. X, p. 70.

8. II Nephi 2:11–16.

9. Benedict de Spinoza, *Ethics* ("Philosophy of Benedict de Spinoza"), trans. R. H. M. Elwes (New York: Tudor Publishing Co., 1936), Pt. I, "Concerning God," Proposition XXIX and Proof of Proposition XXXIII.

10. Philo Judaeus, *Works of Philo Judaeus*, trans. C. D. Yonge (London: George Bell and Sons, 1890), I, 196–97.

11. William James, *Pragmatism* (New York: Longmans Green & Co., 1946), Lec. II, p. 72.

12. B. H. Roberts, *The Gospel* (7th ed.; Salt Lake City: Deseret Book Co., 1928), pp. 106–07.

13. B. H. Roberts, *A Comprehensive History of the Church of Jesus Christ of Latter-day Saints, Century I* (Salt Lake City: Deseret News Press, 1930), II, 399.

14. B. H. Roberts, *Joseph Smith the Prophet Teacher* (Salt Lake City: Deseret News, 1908), p. 49.

15. *Ibid.*, p. 59.

16. B. H. Roberts, *The Mormon Doctrine of Deity* (Salt Lake City: Deseret News, 1903), p. 126.

Part V

1. St. Thomas Aquinas, *The Summa Theologica*, English Dominican translation, rev. Anton C. Pegis, *Basic Writings of Saint Thomas Aquinas*, ed. Anton C. Pegis (New York: Random House, 1945), I. q. 2, a. 3.

2. William Pepperell Montague, *Belief Unbound* (New Haven: Yale University Press, 1930), p. 7.

3. Aristotle, *Metaphysica*, Bk. XII, chap. VII, 10721b, trans. W. D. Ross, *The Works of Aristotle*, eds. J. A. Smith and W. D. Ross (Oxford: Clarendon Press, 1912).

4. Alfred North Whitehead, *Science and the Modern World* (New York: Macmillan Co., 1926), p. 249.

5. Bordon P. Bowne, *Metaphysics* (rev. ed.; New York: American Book Company, 1910), pp. 422, 425.

6. F. H. Bradley, *Appearance and Reality* (London: Swan Sonmenschein & Co., Ltd., 1908), pp. 531, 533.

7. Boethius, *De Duab Nat.*, III, quoted by St. Thomas Aquinas, *The "Summa Theologica" of St. Thomas Aquinas*, literally trans. Fathers of the English Dominican Province (London: Burns, Oates, & Washbourne, Ltd., 1920), I, q. 29, a. 1.

8. St. Thomas Aquinas, *The "Summa Theologica" of St. Thomas Aquinas*, literally trans. Fathers of the English Dominican Province (London: Burns, Oates, & Washbourne, Ltd., 1920), I, q. 29, a. 3.

9. Hermann Lotze, *Outlines of the Philosophy of Religion* (Boston: Ginn and Company, 1886), p. 69.

10. Bradley, *op. cit.*, p. 533.

11. *Ibid.*, pp. 532 f.

12. Karl Barth, *Doctrine of the Word of God*, trans. G. T. Thompson (New York: Charles Scribner's Sons, 1936), p. 157.

13. Martin Buber, *Eclipse of God* (New York: Harper and Brothers, 1957), pp. 60, 96, 97.

14. Paul Tillich, *Systematic Theology* (Chicago: University of Chicago Press, 1951), I, 243 f.

15. *Ibid.*, p. 245.

16. Sarvepalli Radhakrishnan, *The Philosophy of Sarvepalli Radhakrishnan*, ed. P. A. Schilpp (New York: Tudor Publishing Co., 1952), p. 796.

17. Cf. Gershom G. Scholem, *Major Trends in Jewish Mysticism* (Jerusalem: Schocken Publishing House, 1941), First Lec.

18. William Pepperell Montague, *Belief Unbound* (New Haven: Yale University Press, 1930), pp. 6, 66, 67.